Train to Outslug the Market

(WHAT TO DO IF UNAFRAID)

MARTIN SOSNOFF

Golden Apples Press
Palm Beach, FL

On the cover...

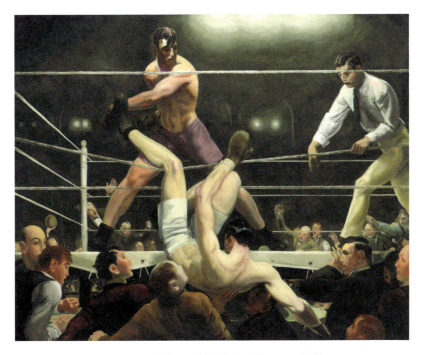

Dempsey and Firpo. 1924, by George Bellows

George Bellows, who I consider one of a dozen great American painters of the 20th century, didn't depict swans paddling majestically in Central Park. One iconic canvas showed Luis Firpo knocking Jack Dempsey through the ropes in a no-holds-barred backroom boxing bout, one of a series held amid the inner seams of old New York.

Here are Bellows' precepts:
- Try everything that can be done.
- Try it every possible way.
- Be deliberate.
- Be spontaneous.
- Be thoughtful and painstaking.
- Be abandoned and impulsive.
- There is nothing I do not want to know that has to do with life or art.
- Revolt against authority and mainstream society.

Copyright © 2020 by Martin Sosnoff

Published in the United States by Golden Apples Press, Palm Beach, FL
All rights reserved. No part of this publication may be used,
reproduced, stored in a retrieval system, or transmitted in any form or by any
means, electronic, mechanical, photocopying, recording,
or otherwise, without written permission of Golden Apples Press.

Library of Congress cataloging-in-publication data available upon request.
ISBN: 978-0-578-76673-7

Project Manager Della R. Mancuso
Designed and composed by Donna Murphy
Graphs prepared by Network Graphics
Chapter opener graphic @ Shutterstock
Printed in Canada
First Edition
9 8 7 6 5 4 3 2 1

For Toni With Love
Always, Totally, Forever

CONTENTS

Graphs, Charts, Illustrations 9

My Streetwise Glossary 11

Introduction: Our $10 Upright—Better Than a Steinway 15

Chapter 1: Become a Smart Self-Centered Investor 19

Chapter 2: No Gilded Age Ahead 25

Chapter 3: Custodial vs. High-Intensity Money Managers 37

Chapter 4: Does Buffett Deserve His Market Premium? 46

Chapter 5: How $5 Stocks Turn into $10 Stocks (Then More) 50

Chapter 6: What to Do if Unafraid 55

Chapter 7: Easy Sell-Down to Your Sleeping Level 62

Chapter 8: Emotional Assets Put Away Venture Capital Returns 68

Chapter 9: The Value Investor's Dilemma (Can't X-Out Growth) 72

Chapter 10: Upward Mobility Is a DIY Process 79

Chapter 11: The Art of Measurement Is Tricky 85

Chapter 12: Polite Exxon Mobil Can Bury You 93

Chapter 13: Boeing's Insidious Art of Discombobulation,
Elon Musk's Greed 98

Chapter 14: Internet and e-Commerce Paper:
Shadow Boxing in the Dark 104

Chapter 15: Junk Bonds Worth Their Weight in Gold 114

Chapter 16: No Nifty Fifty—Pick Half a Dozen 123

Chapter 17: Entry Points Count 130

Chapter 18: The Innermost Game of Investing 134

Chapter 19: Flee Grandiosity, the Killer White Whale 143

Chapter 20: My Dive-Bombing White Swans 148

Chapter 21: Trump, the Murphy Man 152

Chapter 22: Obtain, Maintain, Then Compound Wealth 156

Chapter 23: Hope I'm Too Pessimistic 160

Conclusion: FRB Wimp-Out Bullish for Growthies? 167

GRAPHS, CHARTS, ILLUSTRATIONS

Dempsey and Firpo. 1924, by George Bellows 3 and Front Cover

Knead, 1995, by Jenny Saville 26

Corporate Tax Rate Changes 29

Typical Asset Allocation 39

Berkshire's Underperformance 45

Berkshire Hathaway's Five Top Holdings 46

Sosnoff's Five Largest Holdings 49

Halliburton's Undulations 51

P/E Ratio vs. Long-Term Treasury Yield Since 1930 59

NASDAQ Composite Index 2000-2014 65

KBW Bank Index 67

Frau Am Strand, 1981, by Georg Baselitz 71

Growth vs. Value Sector Comparisons 75

Weighting of Critical Value Factors 76

Percentage of Offspring Earning More Than Parents 80

Dow Jones Industrials Top 10 Market Capitalizations—July 2020 85

Dow Jones Industrials Top 10 Market Capitalizations—December 2014 87

NASDAQ-100 10 Largest Positions—July 2020 88

Top 25 Stocks in the S&P 500 Index—March 31, 2001 90

S&P 500 Sector Weightings 92

Exxon Mobil Price Chart 95

Compensation of Executive Officers 101

Tech's Five-Year Price Run 104

Morgan Guaranty's Portfolio Largest Holdings—Yearend 1972 111

Companies Persisting in Growth Stock Universe 112

Thirty-Year Treasury Bond Yield 118

Disbelief in Growth Surfaced in 2013–2014 127

Thirty-Year S&P 500 Index Valuation Range 142

World Trade Center, NY 143

Ten-Year Treasury Bond Yield 166

MY STREETWISE GLOSSARY

Activist – Began as a greenmailer, now commanding more capital. Respected in boardrooms, even by the *Wall Street Journal*. Carl Icahn.

Amazon.com – Either the next Pan American Airways, killed by its ambition, or a speculator's dream.

Balance Sheet – What nobody cares about until a company is on the brink of bankruptcy, excepting junk bond players.

Book Value – What nobody ever cared about—except Larry Tisch and Warren Buffett.

Discounted Cash Flow – What analysts use to justify stocks that sell at outrageous valuations.

Downside Surprise – A quarterly occurrence.

EBITDA – What analysts use to justify stocks that sell at outrageous valuations.

Equity Risk Premium – Another way of valuing the market through the rear-view mirror. When stocks go up, academics reason why the equity risk premium should go to zero (Dow 36,000). When stocks decline (Black Monday), everyone believes the equity risk premium was too low.

Executive Compensation – Don't ask. Read the proxy document and vote no.

Fed Watching – What to do so you know what will be in their brains 12 months out.

Free Cash Flow – What analysts and some businessmen use to justify properties that sell at outrageous valuations or discounts. Free cash flow above a 6% yield gets my attention.

GAAP vs. Non-GAAP – Serious accounting distinctions nobody cares to deal with.

Greenspeak – What Treasury bond futures discounted three months in advance, although always indecipherable.

Guidance – What management hands out to lazy analysts. The objective is to get 100 analysts projecting earnings within a penny of each other. Management then beats the consensus by a penny. This makes the stock go up—as in Intel.

Index Funds – A *Consumer Reports* "Best Buy."

Irrational Exuberance – A speculative way of life that Alan Greenspan disdained but John Maynard Keynes embraced and took advantage of as a commodities trader.

Long-Term Buy – How analysts denote a stock that is likely to remain doggy for years and years.

Market Technician – Someone who writes opinions on his wife's ironing board. Also an oxymoron.

Metrics – Shorthand for income statement analysis inclusive of gross margins, revenue growth, cash flow and pretax earnings. A company has good or bad metrics based on quarterly comparisons.

Money Market Fund – The worst place to put your money maybe for five years longer.

NASDAQ – A gigantic car wash emporium that uses dirty water and normally humbles its users.

Neutral – How analysts classify a stock that is nearly a disaster.

Private Equity Operators – What savvy politicians yearn to be after leaving office.

S&P 500 Index – What almost everyone is measured against because it's easy to beat, sometimes.

Sequential Growth – Quarter-over-quarter growth rather than year-over-year comparisons. Stocks that sell at 80 times earnings or more must demonstrate sequential growth of 15% or better. Otherwise, they dive off your screen. (No company can do this for more than a couple of years.)

Sombrero Formation – NASDAQ and Greece's roller coaster trajectories from the bubble top.

Stock Picker's Market – Nobody has the foggiest idea what happens next. Good luck, schmuck!

The Takeaway – After a lengthy and discursive session with management, analysts leave with a new spin to the earnings outlook. (It can be positive or neutral, never negative, but definitely what management wants you to take away.)

The Triple Top – What the market fought for 14 years and then broke out of, to everyone's surprise.

Upside Surprise – A very rare occurrence.

VIX – A dumb indicator of sentiment options traders and market technicians follow despite its many sudden reversals.

Volatility – A way of life. Also, what made George Soros superrich.

INTRODUCTION

Our $10 Upright— Better Than a Steinway

Lemme tell you about the Sosnoff family's most precious possession during the Great Depression. It was a scratched-up, black, upright, no-name piano. Our family of five hung around it and sang in unison, my mother sight-reading borrowed sheet music: "South of the Border Down Mexico Way," "Alexander's Ragtime Band," and "You Smile and the Angels Sing." The poor helped each other during the Depression. It was an underground economy, unknown and unmentioned by economists.

Our piano was deadly flat on bass notes and sharp on treble keys, but so what? It functioned fine for the Sosnoffs. We lived in the East Bronx, three flights up—a walk-up tenement, one among hundreds.

Once school let out late in June, my parents gave up our apartment. The family summered in a tar-papered shack at Croton-on-Hudson. We overlooked Indian Point Park, then a sandy beach the color and consistency of brown sugar.

I'm talking late thirties, early forties. Nuclear power generation wasn't even a concept then. We owned so few cumbersome possessions that the New York Central Railroad allowed us to board with all our clothes and baseball bats. My mother lugged on board her 30-pound Underwood typewriter.

But, what to do with our piano? Well…I and my two older brothers, Gene and George, were in charge of moving this beloved monster down to a neighbor's apartment on the ground floor, its home for the summer. The poor took care of each other during the Depression, a seldom remarked sidelight. The corner candy store took our phone messages. Phones were beyond our means until 1946.

Over the years, the three brothers evolved into a handy mover team of non-Steinway instruments. There was actually a moving van enterprise then named "The Four Brothers." We'd upend this object, tip it back and shove a dolly underneath to receive our baby. Amid fulsome cursing and much sweat equity, maybe an hour finished the job.

In early September, the return trip for our piano, up three flights, took several hours. Very dangerous if the dolly slipped out. Somehow, we managed not to self-destruct. It was unthinkable to turn our piano loose like a mangy dog never to be seen again.

When I was nine, my father walked me over to a second-story music school on 125th Street, three blocks south of his tailor shop. There, Pop bought me my choice of a nickel-plated alto saxophone, priced at $35. Pop paid for my sax a buck a week and contracted for weekly music lessons at 25 cents the half hour. Above the music school, on the third floor, a tap dance studio's class rapped out its rhythms, all of us striving upward in a dismal economic setting.

Around this time, New York's greatest mayor, Fiorello LaGuardia, somehow scrounged the money to create four special high schools, including the Bronx High School of Science and the High School of Music and Art, which I later attended, mid-forties. If it weren't for M&A, I would have graduated from a young punk into a hood. There was no such concept as a teenager then.

Music, the theater, all the arts were a must-do in our family. My elder brother, Gene, took me to the old Metropolitan Opera House where standing-room admission was one buck in the late forties. You could sit in the third balcony of Broadway's theaters for $1.10. *Life with Father* played along with Ethel Merman belting out "Anything You Can Do, I Can Do Better" in *Annie Get Your Gun.*

Decades later, Steinway Industries accepted a private equity bid of $438 million, over one times sales. Steinways now retail new anywhere from $57,000 to $142,000. Average income of buyers tops $300,000.

We just bought a Steinway Model M, circa 1916, mahogany, $45,000

Our $10 Upright—Better Than a Steinway

reconstructed. My annual income is unprovable. At the National Museum of American Illustration, a labor of love by Judy and Lawrence Cutler, in Newport, RI, I noted a painting by Hamilton King, *Lady at the Piano*.

This was transformed into a 1900 illustration by the Victoria Greeting Card Company. A tall drink of water gowned in floor-length velvet and lace, a coiffed Gibson Girl hairdo, legs outstretched languorously. The subject touched the keys with her fingertips. Beautiful women at pianos resonate.

In my late teens, I made sideman in a name dance band with a five-man sax section. I had traded in my nickel-plated sax for a sweet-toned Selmer. The parent, actually Selmer, acquired Steinway in 1995. I didn't blink at the $200 price tag for a Selmer because I had to have a Selmer to survive in the music world.

What in the world do pianos and saxophones signify for financial markets? Actually, plenty. Objects and services that enrich your emotional life hold their primacy just so long as quality remains impeccably high. Steinways hand-crafted a hundred years ago adumbrate wonderful tonality, soft to the touch, still highly competitive with new models.

When I scan my portfolio, daily, each position must spell viability. I'm disinterested in commodity plays unless they're giving 'em away, bordering on insolvency, what we had early 2020. I long for properties with great cancer drugs, electric pickup trucks, e-commerce and cloud computing capacity. Primacy in media content and distribution get my attention like Walt Disney and T-Mobile. Microsoft is my biggest holding, for now.

My pursuit of excellence, not perfection, proved elusive but was ingrained early on.

Become a Smart Self-Centered Investor

When I go to the Great Barn in the sky, I've left instructions for my family trust funds and endowments. No banks. No Buffetts. An S&P Index fund is allocated 50% of assets. The NASDAQ-100 gets 20%, and the remaining 30% is spread between a couple of high-yield ETFs. Anyone who has a high-yield ETF at the least should get their proxy statement to see how assets are diversified.

Can you fight the battle for investment survival? **If a passive player, your biggest decision isn't which bank or brokerage house you choose to manage your assets. It's portfolio structure as to fixed income assets and equities,** not whether the yen is a better play than the dollar or pound.

Unlike Princess Aurora in *Sleeping Beauty*, the average investor won't ever encounter some handsome prince awakening one with a kiss after a long slumber and then you live happily ever after. Inequality flourishes. The amplitude between winners and losers among the 25 largest capitalizations grows wider. General Electric, U.S. Steel, AT&T, Ford Motor and Exxon Mobil stood as horrid performers for years. Nobody ever expected General Electric to sell down to $5.

The armchair investor can learn a lot upon considering a few macros applied to his stock holdings. First, is there a theme in his portfolio—growth, value, high dividends, materials producers? Are your holdings subject to the forces of inflation or deflation? Are you buying management dynamics or an executive group that goes through all the motions of running the business, year after year, just reacting to the business cycle? If you're a random stock picker you need to

Train to Outslug the Market

stop. Your luck won't hold out.

In securities markets, life is unfair. There can be decades of zero returns. After the tech bubble of 2000, it took NASDAQ 15 years to recover. Aside from personal fortunes made by the Koch brothers in petrochemicals—maybe $100 billion—Jeff Bezos, Bill Gates and Mark Zuckerberg have benefited from richly capitalized earnings in their publicly traded stock. For internet and e-commerce houses, we're talking about outsized multiples of earnings, EBITDA and operating cash flow. Lopsided valuation made them plutocrats—Koch brothers excepted, because they've shunned going public. Facebook sells at six times book value.

Passive investors must face the fact that action is bewildering on the Big Board where share volume of 700 million is normal. Late fifties, I remember three to four million shares was a normal day. The American Exchange then stayed open Saturday mornings to gather in some more business for its members.

For certain, Louis XVI, Czar Nicholas II, even Cleopatra believed in income inequality as well. The Czar was conveyed in a solid gold chariot. My father, cranking a mimeograph machine in the 1905 revolution, was caught by the Czar's police and jailed for a year.

Our country has staggered through horrendous financial events touched off by the Cuban Missile Crisis, 9/11, the tech bubble, Volcker's 15% interest-rate invocation and the 2008–2009 financial meltdown. COVID-19's havoc is the equivalent of 2008–2009.

Invariably, in panics, the market sells down to 10 times earnings and yields 5% at book value. Before COVID-19 hit early months in 2020, the S&P 500 Index sold at twice book value, yielded maybe 2% and carried a price-earnings multiplier of 18 times forward 12-months earnings. At yearend 2019, punditry waxed bullish. Even bank stocks rallied sharply on expectations of rising interest rates bolstering their net-interest margin on loans outstanding. But by mid-2020 Treasury rates hovered near zero, even for 10-year paper.

A review of past decade performance of Berkshire Hathaway is instructive. Warren Buffett underperformed his rated index, the S&P 500, because he was overweighted not just in bank stocks, some 40% of investments, but virtually the entire portfolio remained in a value construct of energy industrials and consumer non-durables like Coca Cola—what Buffett has stuck to for 60-odd years.

But, past decade, actually from 2007, growth put away value investing. The Russell 1000 Growth Index beat Russell 1000 Value by 4.3 percentage points, annually, an enormous variance. Buffett eschewed the Facebooks and Amazons as beyond his zone of valuation. They were unmappable, overpriced, but sought after by rest-of-world.

Are you in-gear or out-of-gear as it applies to the business cycle's variance in GDP, inflation, FRB policy reversals and the drift in geopolitical conflicts? **Believe me, you'll never get any help from economic forecasts made by the Federal Reserve, the International Monetary Fund and Wall Street punditry.** They all invariably miss inflection points on macroeconomic forces driving change in the world. In short, your guess is as good as their pedantry. From quarter to quarter, they try to catch up to change at the margin by revising their numbers going forward.

Conceptually, you want to own stocks good for the next 50 years, but if what you own is underperforming for two to four quarters, don't lapse into passivity or rationalization. Other elements, like balance-sheet analysis, can tell you whether the company in question is too leveraged with debt. If so, you own a junk bond, not a stock. There are entire industries leveraged with debt that I'd consider uninvestable. Airlines, for example, but also automobiles, as in Ford Motor, even General Motors. In retailing, Marshall Field's and J.C. Penney failed but not Costco and Walmart. I love Costco's price-points for hearing aid batteries.

At the least, appreciate products and services offered by the companies you invest in—American Express, but not Wells Fargo. I'm talking about Apple, Procter & Gamble, Coca-Cola, PepsiCo and Merck. If you can, follow changes in market share, product pricing and innovation. *Consumer Reports* is a must-read.

In normal times, huge federal deficits prompted the Fed to raise interest rates unrelentingly. But deflationary forces in today's world seem more 'n' more entrenched. Zero or near-zero interest rates, even negative numbers prevailed for years in Japan and parts of Europe with no signs of an upbeat as yet in such economies.

Deflation in the commodity sector is more 'n' more pervasive. The world is awash in oil and gas surpluses with flattish demand. Commodities like steel, iron ore, copper and aluminum likewise can remain in a surplus condition. Stocks like Alcoa, Halliburton, U.S. Steel and Occidental Petroleum faded badly, their comeback conjectural. You're speculating in commodity futures, by owning them. Halliburton is my play.

Economists abhor deflationary constructs of low interest rates, minimal inflation and sloppy commodity prices. Academics fear deflation reduces consumer spending. Nobody buys in advance if prices stay flattish. Major sectors like automobiles, appliances and apparel come to mind. This is academic nonsense. Everyday low prices stimulate consumer spending.

Look at housing. Mortgage rates at 3% for single-family homes do trigger refinancing and incremental demand. But housing as a percentage of GDP isn't a dominant sector. There's a reason not to fear flattish GDP, because personal-consumption expenditures should hold up, at 70% of our GDP. Everything else, like the trade balance, gross private investment (capital spending) and inventories are smaller sectors, volatile and unpredictable, quarter by quarter.

If you believe as I do that low interest rates last a couple more years along with some commodity deflation, it dictates a reallocation of equity assets over several sectors of the market. You don't want much money in oil and gas properties. Same goes for commodities like steel, aluminum, copper and iron ore. Exxon Mobil was a doggy stock making new lows for years. Halliburton got crushed, from $29 a share to five bucks, where it was a steal unless you forecast a wipeout. Oil futures bounced and the stock doubled in a month.

Top five names in the S&P 500 five years ago comprised just 11% of weighting. Currently, we're over 20%. Internet and e-commerce babies run nearly twice as volatile as the market, both ways. The list stands or falls on their performance. The NASDAQ-100 Index is the way to play the tech sector. In a

Becoming a Smart Self-Centered Investor

bull market NASDAQ outperforms all other indices.

Never underestimate violent change in markets or cumulative change. Consider, Johnson & Johnson and Exxon Mobil as well as Berkshire Hathaway were in 2014's top five names. Wells Fargo was number six and General Electric sat in seventh place. Meanwhile, Facebook and Alphabet held near bottom positions in the top 25 listing.

I doubled back to track price-earnings ratios over 50 years. The market traded at 18 times earnings in 1972, but a deep real-estate recession crushed stocks in 1973–1974. In 2000 the index exceeded 20 times, while yearend 2014 we ticked at 17 times earnings. Starkly, 1972 premiums for growth ranged up to four times the market, but not for long. The deep recession in 1973–1974 plus worldwide competitive forces collapsed earnings for Polaroid, Xerox, Avon Products and Eastman Kodak. They never came back.

Lemme use the dangerous phrase "today it's different." There's no Japanese or Chinese company that can stand up to Facebook, Microsoft, Alphabet and Apple. Certainly, Alibaba is a prospective challenger to Amazon in e-commerce and I own it. R&D productivity at Facebook, Apple, Microsoft and Alphabet are determinants of future long-term growth rates. Who knows? What you can say is these four growthies plow back heady percentages of revenues in R&D. We'll soon see whether they're throwing away their money.

Net, net, low interest rates favor growth stocks. Only a deep recession kills them off by crushing P/E ratios and earnings. Not my call. I've rethought my overweighted position in the financial sector, namely banks, and banged them out. There's no case for rising net-interest margins so no leverage in operating earnings. While the price-earnings ratio for bank stocks, particularly Citigroup, stands near 60% of the S&P 500 Index, I'd expect no near-term closing of the valuation discount.

Remember, historically, a low interest-rate setting favors growth stocks. Technology can reign as the dominant sector of the S&P 500 Index, now over 25%. Maybe headed to 30%.

Today, the market is dominated by a handful of tech and internet houses, namely Microsoft, Alphabet, Amazon, Facebook and Apple. Fifteen years ago, General Electric held primacy with a market capitalization of $415 billion while Exxon Mobil was number three at $280 billion. Citigroup was number five. American International Group in seventh place at $186 billion became a basket case in the 2008–2009 financial meltdown. Citigroup needed a reverse split to regain double-digit price status. Mid-2020, it was Chesapeake Energy's turn to play the overleveraged victim of declining oil quotes with a reverse split.

Passive investors should avoid at all times overleveraged companies, whether it be in energy, retailing, financials or airlines. They do tap out. I can't figure out Boeing's source and application of funds next couple of years, so I stay away from it. Big tech houses are flooded with cash, little or no debt and sell at definable numbers on operating cash flow.

The passive investor should at the least understand macro forces governing broad industry sectors that get his money. Get that right and everything else falls into place—earnings, price-earnings ratios, even dividends and Wall Street favor.

If anything, financial markets are turning even more volatile because of huge concentrations of invested assets in specific industry ETF sectors like oil, technology, financials, high-yield bonds, as well. NASDAQ-100 I'd treat as an emotional asset, worth going against the grain for its extremities.

If referencing the market against the Dow Jones Industrials, you're obsolete, still living in the dark ages of the 1950s. Technology as a market sector then was insignificant.

No Gilded Age Ahead

Upfront, I need to tell a story on myself. Maybe it was 1982 when Jean-Michel Basquiat left the streets of New York City as a graffiti activist. Basquiat was holed up in the basement of a West Broadway gallery, painting furiously some 14 hours a day.

I got a call from Mary Boone, a prominent dealer who had sold me several new pieces by German neo-expressionists like Kiefer, Baselitz, Immendorff and Penck. I've held them for nearly 40 years, collecting art like Warren Buffett collects stocks. His American Express holding dates back to 1964.

Basquiat's 1982 canvases were wildly psychedelic, colorist pieces. Swish, swish went the paint strokes, geometrically angulated with references to his heroes in the jazz world, baseball, whatever. The back-and-forth with Mary went like this: "You better buy a couple," Mary urged me. "They're $2,500 apiece."

"Mary," I said, "why are you bothering me with this work? I'll admit, Basquiat has some possibilities, but my focus now is on the new German work that's just come over here."

Well, nearly 40 years later, one of these Basquiats sold at auction for $100 million. Sooo…I could've bought half a dozen Basquiats and made half a billion. But, cavalierly, I turned my nose up at 'em.

Think of it! I wouldn't still be reading myself blind over annual reports, 10Qs, 10Ks, proxy statements and 50 pages daily of Wall Street's music sheets. What they call institutional research.

Train to Outslug the Market

I'll insert here an image of a Jenny Saville canvas painted in 1995. It's a portrait of a woman exiting surgery for facial work, the oxygen tube still inserted in her mouth. Her bloated face, swollen, black and blue, sucked me in. I bought it after it was "passed" at a London auction.

Knead, 1995, by Jenny Saville.
© 2020 Artists Rights Society (ARS), New York / DACS, London.

I never asked Jenny whether she agreed with me, that the piece's theme was what women do to themselves these days to remain competitive. That's why I fell in love with it, first sight. A decade later, Saville's "ugly" paintings surged into great demand by collectors, up 1,000%. Lest we forget, Manet's *Olympia* sparked a public scandal, but now rests comfortably in the Louvre Museum.

No Gilded Age Ahead

Money management is like art collecting. First, you need to be early on and an in-depth player to build a collection (portfolio). Perception counts in both disciplines. It can't be taught past a certain point, so everyone wrestles with the tiger, repeatedly.

Personally, I abhor a wealth tax on my assets, which didn't benefit from a capitalized value multiplier. I've already paid over 60 years of taxes on interest income, dividends and capital gains. For me, the wealth tax is a redundant levy.

Consider: Bill Gates, Jeff Bezos and Warren Buffett along with multibillionaires like Eli Broad favor a wealth tax or have earmarked almost all their net worth to their foundations. These gestures fall short of what the country needs. After all, GDP is measured in tens of trillions.

I say this after submerging myself in over 60 years of macro statistics covering the country's waxing and waning, its tax structure and lack of same. Market panics going back to the Cuban Missile Crisis, the Fed's pressure on interest rates in 1982, the 2000 tech bubble and the financial meltdown of 2008–2009 pressed market operators like me, but I always came back. The middle class hardly squeezed by.

Nobody's to blame for the middle class languishing in their unhappy, dreary wealth-share cohort. You can't fault our federal tax structure for being confiscatory. Offshore competition capped industrial wages in the U.S. It's cheaper to make cars in Mexico.

The average American carries most of his wealth in his home. Yes. They may hold $100,000 or so in financial assets, but they can't tap this capital until retirement. There's little delegated control over assets in pension and profit-sharing funds.

I remember the Great Depression and my father's tailor shop in Harlem, where the pressing machine gurgled hot air. Max, the presser in his T-shirt, would mumble "I am too poor to live and too poor to die." As a 10-year-old I had no idea I was poor, belonging to the underclass. After all, my parents were too proud to go on "relief," the equivalent of today's food stamps. I had a snappy throwing arm from third base, a big deal in the schoolyard.

Train to Outslug the Market

Last time I looked, 46 million recipients got food stamps, the individual stipend around $144, monthly. I'm sensitive to safety nets. In my early twenties, I came back from the Korean War in 1954, unemployed. My insurance stipend ran $25 weekly for 20 weeks. We called it the "25-20 Club."

Today, there's pervasive genteel poverty with student loans averaging $25,000, but 10 times more for medical school graduates. Congress in its infinite wisdom put an adjustable interest clause on this debt. Prospective borrowing costs could easily escalate to 6% or 7%, presently 3.5%.

Net, net, the middle class's problem is a structural condition defying any near-term fix. State and local employment has peaked out because tax receipts don't grow. The construction industry lost two million jobs from peak to trough in 2007–2009. Only low-paying jobs like food service and the hospital sector show some growth, but this is mainly part-timers, with no medical or pension benefits.

Payrolls in manufacturing sadly spell out the demise of our competitive mettle compared with low-cost zones in South America and the Far East. U.S. manufacturing employment peaked in the late seventies near 20 million. The biggest decline came in the past decade. We're based out close to the 12 million worker level.

As a percentage of nonagricultural employees, manufacturing is basing out near 10% compared with its early postwar peak of 33%. The plight of our skilled workforce population in terms of earnings gains is insidious, at 2% per annum, down from 4% 20 years ago. The days of the 8% wage bumps in the seventies are gone, forever. Ask Teamsters and UAW honchos. In financial markets, there're decades of zero returns. It took NASDAQ 15 years to recover from its tech-bubble high set in 2000. Today, Microsoft sells at 25 times forward year's earnings, Facebook at seven times book value. How's that for disparity?

Surely, the minimum wage in the country is too low, even at $15 an hour. There are tens of millions of part-timers in retailing, food and medical services. They barely get by, underpaid, uninsured and easily terminated. Healthcare costs for wage earners are eating them alive, annually rising in double digits.

No Gilded Age Ahead

CORPORATE TAX RATE CHANGES

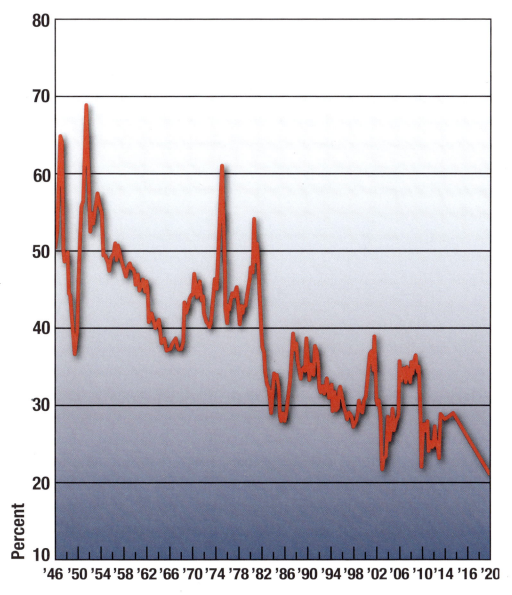

Figure 1
Source: Department of Commerce

Without redress, healthcare insurance can take a 50% bite out of middle-class income. Remember your compound interest tables. Compound 10% and it doubles in six and a half years. There's no gilded age in store for more than 100,000 plutocrats extant.

There are ways to raise tax receipts without attacking existing wealth. When I arrived on Wall Street in 1959, stock commissions counted up to 1% on a round lot with no break on volumetric trades. That world ended in the seventies with negotiated commissions.

If you want to know who the country is being run for, just look at the sharp, downward slope in the corporate tax rate during the entire span of postwar decades. We've gone from 70% in the early postwar years to the mid-twenties of late.

Now, everyone trades for pennies per share, perhaps one-hundredth of what it cost decades ago. We need to see a tax on share trading, much of which is pure speculation by professionals rather than individual investors. The Street can scream bloody murder, but so what? In the sixties, I remember share volume at 3 to 4 million on an average day.

Today, 700-million share days are common. On a 250-day trading year, let's tack on a fee of 0.5%. For a 100-share trade at $50 the tax would be $25, manageable for a long-term investor. For traders scalping eighths and quarters, it's onerous and could impact market liquidity. But, per annum, it can raise $50 billion in tax revenues, not attacking wealth directly but some of the cost of getting rich.

I'm a ragpicker in under-$10 plays, companies that haven't been discounted as yet. It could be in biotechnology, a tech house, even a small operator in a relatively new industry like cellular telephony a decade ago.

Nextel was called to my attention by my son, Scott, who worked there in long-range planning and pricing subscriptions for cellular hookups. Nextel traded at $4 a share then. Nobody cared because of conservative projections in cellular usage and ultimate saturation levels as a percentage of households.

Everyone believed the saturation level for cellular would top out at 10% of U.S. households. Cellular phones were just too expensive, running up to

No Gilded Age Ahead

$300. Of course, the industry blew through such nonsensical projections. We're now over 100% saturation with some families buying phones for their preteen children.

Until Nextel as a stock moved into low teens, analysts ignored it because its market capitalization was minimal, under a billion, a small-capitalization piece of paper. I ended up selling Nextel at $34 when they were about to be acquired by Sprint just a few years later.

Wall Street's analysts forever refuse to delve into the widening gap between GAAP and non-GAAP reported earnings, particularly for tech houses.

Coming redistribution of wealth next decade? I'd put it no more than 1%. If you've got $100 million, it will cost you a million. If it's levied per annum, all hell breaks loose, with enormous negative consequences to GDP.

If the Democrats regain control of Congress, a wealth tax is coming. I like taxing unrealized gains of the guys in T-shirts worth tens of billions. At the least, it will accelerate capital movement to their foundations, a good thing.

The first lesson I learned as a player is nothing's forever; maybe five to 10 years is all you may gain. Secondly, if you're a poor boy from the East Bronx, you thirst to use leverage, even on a 10-to-1 basis. Donald Trump did this as a real estate developer, but tapped out on untimely plays in gaming casinos. Yes, he leveraged his name, and built Trump Tower, but Equitable Life Assurance held more equity. His was a minority interest.

In the fifties I knew families with $1 cost on their IBM, but later IBM lost its competitive edge and needed to be saved by an outsider, Lou Gerstner. Great stocks like Xerox, Polaroid, even Avon Products and Eastman Kodak turned into also-rans and then saw the sun set on their prostrate bodies.

Warren Buffett substituted perception for leverage. Be early in perceiving where a company's franchise, new product development and pricing primacy can take it. Buffett fell in love with newspapers like the Washington Post, but later the internet intervened. Today this newspaper is owned by Jeff Bezos as a vanity kind of holding. You can afford this when your net worth mushrooms past a hundred billion. Security analysts with 30-page research reports will never make you rich. On the way up and down, they're invariably late in their perception, what we term lagging indicators.

Here's another example of using extraordinary leverage in an industry at the takeoff stage: The birth of jet aircraft in 1960 by both Boeing and Douglas Aircraft unleashed productivity gains for all the airlines that then lived from hand to mouth. You could now span the Atlantic and Pacific in seven or eight hours for maybe $300 on charter. Suddenly, monthly airline revenues sprinted ahead 25% to 30%. I flew to Honolulu, then a beautiful backwater with a couple of small first-class hotels like the Royal Hawaiian. Not rich enough or knowledgeable about real estate, I coulda bought up half of Bishop Street for a song.

I did the next best thing. A couple of airlines—Boeing and United Aircraft—had outstanding convertibles trading near par. So I tapped a money broker who gave me 10-to-1 leverage. I'd put up 10 points on a convertible selling near par. Then marked to market, daily, but never called for more margin. Eastern Airlines converts reached $400 in a couple of years. Boeing's head of commercial aircraft gave me a bicycle to tour the plant in Renton, WA, where I learned about the initial use of titanium fasteners, thereby uncovering a whole new sector of metallurgy for my research.

Another aggressive investment gambit has to do solely with the market cycle, which can be viciously abrupt, both ways. Here's where your quotient of courage gets measured. When there's panic in the streets, the pendulum always swings too far. I go back to the early sixties. Remember the Cuban Missile Crisis, the 1973–1974 real estate debacle, then 1982's Federal Reserve Board press to 15% interest rates. Throw in the tech bubble of 2000, Black Monday in 1987 and then the truly scary financial meltdown of 2008–2009.

At the bottom, I bought Lehman Brothers at $4 a share and Bank of America preferred stock at $5. Lehman tanked, but Bank of America's preferred fought its way back to $25.

Nobody's perfect. **You never want to get fixated on one piece of paper.** Rather, carry several categories of investment at the bottom of any cycle. For me, today, it's supergrowth internet and e-commerce stocks, but I own as well a bunch of ragamuffins selling under $10 a share that I believe are survivors and great cyclical recovery prospects.

Wealth should unfold as a byproduct of what you do and how you think. Never accept the romantic fallacy that striking it rich is possible. Acting on outsiders' stock tips is a sure road to disaster. After all, the guy giving you free advice may change his mind tomorrow, but forget to call you with the news. Never assume the guy on the other end of the phone is smarter than you.

Warren Buffett, for example, proved single-minded in his belief that owning companies with franchise power was a core concept. It helped he was an early-on implementer. I'm thinking of positions held decade-over-decade. Short-listed were American Express, Coca-Cola and the *Washington Post*, even Wells Fargo, which I hate for misusing its clientele with fees drawn out of the open air.

Being early is equivalent to a low entry point. Then, you monitor your animal's performance against the market and its stock grouping. If your paper underperforms comparable paper, say Ford Motor vs. General Motors or Facebook vs. Alphabet, sell off the also-rans. Time horizon no more than one year.

The converse is often overlooked. On good-acting stocks, hold your position. If Halliburton bounces from $5 and change to $11, compare its move with Schlumberger and maybe broaden your sector commitment. Belief in a management's competence is an overriding issue.

Call me a risk taker who employed mountains of leverage that worked out. Wrong-footed, I'd be a wipeout. Early sixties, I could accommodate ultimate risk as a young player with low overhead. I needed just a desk, telephone and yellow pad. The comeback kid carried low overhead.

Misguided courage can destroy you practically overnight. First off, deal with the financial structure of your life. You need earnings power that provides some residual capital. Education counts because it opens up job opportunities that hopefully turn open-ended. Talent on Wall Street is recognized early on. Consider, making serious money operating in financial markets is the hardest work, bar none.

Ironically, the rich can churn their stock market money capriciously. My naïve notion that the wealthier you become, the more intensive is your research, proved a romantic fallacy. As for crowd behavior, I remember James Thurber's piece on when he was an ROTC cadet. His company was in the throes of close order drill with the colonel rattling off like a machine gun: "Right flank march, left flank march, to the rear march." Then the colonel said "right turn march," which is a helluva different command. The entire company marched off in a flanking movement while Thurber found himself alone in a right turn. "You're all wrong and this man's right," the colonel yelled out. So much for crowd behavior.

When Edwin Land, headman at Polaroid, ignored competitive forces from Sony and Nikon, while his research turned fallow, I got off the Polaroid bus. The greatest growth stock of the fifties turned into dust. Does anybody but me remember their low-cost Swinger model? Land projected that everyone in the world would carry one on his shoulder. It reminds me of Mark Zuckerberg's Facebook goal: reaching the entire world population as Facebook users. Zuck's halfway there.

Here are historic markers that matter:
- **Stocks do better than bonds over a 25- to 50-year time span.**
- **Volatility of fixed income investments easily can match equities in both directions.**
- **The market (S&P 500 Index) can sell at book value, sometimes two times book. Yields can range from 1% to 5%, or 6% at the bottom of a cycle.**
- **Ten-year Treasuries, September 2020, yielded 0.6%, but in 1982 during FRB tightening yielded 15%. Five-year paper ranged in the same trajectory.**
- **Inflation, now imperceptible, under 1%, rose to 8% early eighties. It made our country uncompetitive, as in General Motors.**
- **Dollar depreciation or appreciation can range minus 25% to plus 25%.**

- Deep-seated financial risk lurks in almost every type of asset. Banks capitalized at $200 billion do self-destruct with bad loans. American International Group needed a government package of $180 billion to remain solvent.

My bedrock investment guidelines:

- Don't own muni paper rated below AA. To mitigate interest-rate risk, keep bond duration averaging under 10 years.
- Be prepared to hold fixed income investments to maturity. Don't put more than 10% of assets in below-investment-grade corporates or in preferred stocks. Almost all preferred stocks are issued by financial corporations like banks and insurance underwriters. At the bottom of the financial meltdown in 2009, Bank of America's preferred sold at $5, sinking from its $25 par value. Citigroup's common stock bottomed at one buck before its 1-for-10 reverse split. Citigroup may not see its 2007 high, $560 adjusted, for the next 50 years, if then.
- Don't retain an investment advisor for stock market participation. Buy an index fund from a reputable house like Fidelity Investments or Vanguard. Make sure their fees, all in, hold under 20 basis points per annum. Your mindset must be to hold index funds throughout a full cycle—as long as five, 10, even 20 years. Don't trade in and out, the sure way to serfdom and self-loathing.
- If conservative, fix on a ratio of half equities, half bonds. In a historically low interest-rate environment (today), hold maturities of no more than five years. If your tax rate is relatively high, municipals normally afford a better after-tax return than corporates and Treasuries. In a low interest-rate setting, markets levitate in tandem with earnings power, approximately 5% to 7% annually, but not a given. Own growth stocks.

Fixed income investments currently aren't competitive with equity markets. The S&P 500 Index, weighted primarily by large-capitalization companies— Apple, Microsoft and Amazon—is the standard of measurement appropriate for passive but serious investors.

The average life of a growth stock rarely lasts over five years. Only a handful prevail a decade or longer. Your image of a corporation's viability and competitive mettle is probably five to 10 years out-of-date. They don't know you own their stock and even love it passionately for its product offerings.

Disregard how I manage my own money. I've big blocks of capital in high-yield debentures. I'm overconcentrated in half a dozen stocks. They are researchable, understandable, liquid and aggressively managed. Leverage is usable for me because today it's cheap to borrow at 70 basis points. In short, I arbitrage money. Mine is a super-volatile group of stocks that trade actively, millions of shares daily. I can bang out all my animals while sipping a cup of java.

Custodial vs. High-Intensity Money Managers

I've great respect for Warren Buffett. After all, he's made more money than I past 60 years. Give him credit for flouting traditional money management prescripts as followed by major banks and investment houses. They manage trillions of assets for wealthy clients with indifferent results. Nobody complains too loudly because imposed conservative benchmarks are easy to keep pace with in most years.

The embedded risk-tolerance standard for most major asset managers is the 60/40 ratio. Stocks, worldwide, are allocated up to 60% of assets, while bonds and assorted asset plays like gold, oil, emerging-market debt and equity sectors get some play.

JPMorgan Chase, for example, follows the traditional pie-chart investment construct—60% equities with 40% in fixed income investments. Wealth management is a major profit center for banks. Quarterly net revenues for Morgan run at a $3.6 billion clip. Earnings power in a good year runs over $3 billion. This high-margined business benefits from scale on a $2.2 trillion asset base. From client to client, everyone's portfolio is analogous if not duplicated.

I remember when personal holding companies invariably sold at steep discounts to asset value. The market busily marked down idiosyncrasies of the high-metabolic achiever who controlled his company and was deemed capable of jumping off the "deep end" with foolish plays. Where have all these operators gone?

Why pay an additional fee here? Conspicuously, Morgan prefers this to allocating, say, 10% of assets to the NASDAQ-100 Index, which has outperformed almost all asset classes by a wide margin. Past 12 months, ending August 2020, it doubled, but just 50% for the S&P 500 Index. I never hear anyone talking about NASDAQ, like it's a dirty word. If Morgan had placed 10% of client portfolios in the NASDAQ-100 past couple of years, they woulda outperformed their benchmarks, but they didn't.

Intricate chop-chop of client portfolios raises the question, like what is the central idea therein? Whose currency waxes stronger for longer? Should passive clients with limited experience in financial markets feel secure that their capital rests in good hands and undergoes intensive management? Maybe yes, maybe no.

In this, the "pie-chart" investment schema, clients never get badly misused. Results rarely outperform or underperform by more than a couple of percentage points. Sitting on investment committees of a couple of endowment funds, I've found myself less than collegial. Past couple of years, Morgan, for example, has underperformed by a couple of percentage points. They used index funds for a percentage of their equity composite and retained a few independent money managers who go for higher rates of return.

I find pie charts denoting where client assets are spread a bewildering concoction. How many investors bring anything to the table for evaluating such asset division? I understand pivotal variables in asset categories like gold, oil, emerging-market debt, offshore equity placement, real estate, even alternative hard assets. But who can judge whether equity placements in Japan or Asia ex-Japan are better than 5% in mid-cap equities?

I like average duration of five years in bond portfolios and very limited investment in banks' preferred stocks and debentures. In the financial cave-in, 2008–'09, Bank of America needed a Buffett bailout and Merrill Lynch was a basket case merged out. Lehman Brothers was forced into liquidation.

How to fight the battle for investment survival? If a passive player, your biggest decision isn't which bank or brokerage house you choose to manage your assets. **It's portfolio structure** as to fixed income assets and equities, not whether the yen is a better play than the dollar or pound.

I leave emerging-market debt paper beyond my zone of comprehension.

Custodial vs. High-Intensity Money Managers

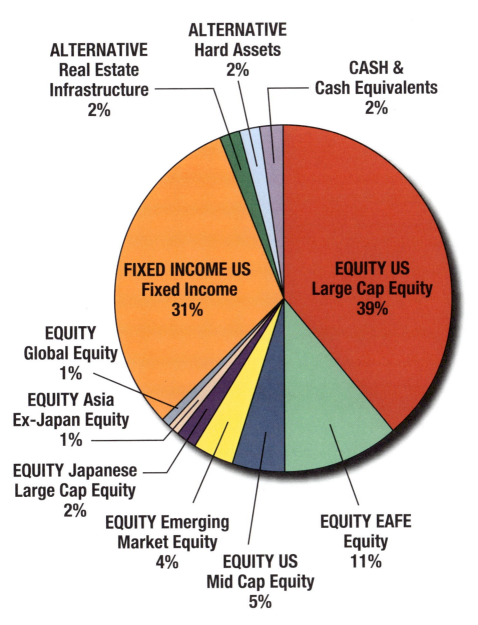

Figure 2

Train to Outslug the Market

If you buy NASDAQ-100, basically you're overweighted in technology and e-commerce. Top five positions account for 45% of the index's weighting. PepsiCo barely makes the list, at 2%. Consider, technology comprises over 25% of the S&P 500's weighting. Another way to construe the NASDAQ-100 is you're double-weighted in technology. While Amazon carries little bottom-line earnings, Microsoft brings down plenty and sells at 1.5 times the multiple of the S&P 500 Index. I'm OK here.

Spring of 2020, I concluded the NASDAQ top 10 were no riskier than the market which sold at 18 times normalized earnings, which were nowhere in sight. Midyear I carried a 14% position in Microsoft, hardly more than its index weighting. This surprised me, but also gave me comfort. Not a totally outlandish bet.

Another way to construe the NASDAQ-100 is you're operating as aggressively weighted as a maximum-intensity hedge fund operator. When I checked latest quarterly 13F filings, there were few operators consistently overweighted in technology. Tiger Global Management, an $18 billion fund, stood out with 30% weighted in Facebook, Microsoft, Amazon and Alibaba. Some 65% of Appaloosa's assets rested in tech houses.

Duquesne's Family Office is practically all tech with special plays, plus a 5% position in General Electric, which mid-2020 traded near its low point. Lone Pine Capital, likewise tech positioned. Top holding was 7% in Alibaba, one of my longs. T. Rowe Price Associates, a long-standing growth stock house, runs a highly diversified portfolio of $771 billion. With the exceptions of Visa and Boeing, the three top positions were Amazon, Microsoft and Facebook.

What's notable is how many high-powered managers turned up noses on Apple. It was as scarce as an energy stock in these portfolios. Big tech rode through the coronavirus tragedy of broad-based industry shutdowns practically unscathed. Amazon and Microsoft, trillion-dollar capitalizations, pushed into all-time high ground. Meantime, AT&T, yielding 7%, went unwanted, 30% off its high. If you're bogged down in Ford Motor and General Electric, think about whether you need more structure in your holdings.

Custodial vs. High-Intensity Money Managers

Quarterly, I scan a couple of dozen 13F reports on independent money managers, looking for groupthink, overspeculation and concentration in specific sectors of the market and in individual stocks. I note what high-metabolic overachievers don't own or over-own. Instead of Apple, they've concentrated on internet and e-commerce stocks that Warren Buffett is allergic to. Namely, Facebook, Amazon, Alphabet and Alibaba. Microsoft, over a $1 trillion market capitalization, also is under-owned by many of the players, a big mistake latest 12 months, since Microsoft has levitated.

Why pay big fees to several money managers who duplicate the NASDAQ-100 Index in their portfolios? This is the case for Tiger Global Management and Coatue Management, Appaloosa Management and Lone Pine Capital. Ironically, Pershing Square Capital Management held a 15% position in Berkshire Hathaway, since sold. Normally, money managers remain allergic to owning other money managers' stock. Why give 'em a leg up? Pershing is a value player so maybe Berkshire fitted into Bill Ackman's portfolio construct.

I went the other way, spring of 2020, with GDP mired by a shut-down country's miasma. I bought more Amazon as my play on the shut-in country. Everyone was light in energy and basic industrials, many missing the market's snappy 20% lifting in May.

I'm a believer in "looking over the valley" on stocks with solid competitive position on the board and sound balance sheets. It got me into Walt Disney and Zoetis but not General Electric, Macy's and Ford Motor. Wish 'em luck.

No problem betting on banks today as a macro play on reflation, but so far it's a nonstarter. Let's see whether loan-loss reserves prove adequate. If not, subtract 20% from bank stock valuation. Before you buy a bank stock, check what happened to it in the 2008–2009 financial meltdown. Citigroup traded near zero before its reverse stock split.

JPMorgan touched down under $20, and didn't recover to its previous $60 high in 2000 until 2015. Gimme a break! Apple past five years has whooshed over 350%. Curiously, sorting through a couple of dozen 13Fs, nobody pounced on Apple like Buffett did. What are all you guys doing in Occidental Petroleum? Carl Icahn sold out his major position in Apple years ago.

Before looking at specific portfolio holdings, check the manager's static ratio, which reveals turnover activity. Appaloosa Management's static ratio was zero, a full turnover. Now, it's pretty much a NASDAQ-100 Index tech portfolio. The usual suspects—Microsoft, Facebook and Amazon. Investors could avoid any management fee content herein, just buying the NASDAQ-100 Index.

Berkshire's static ratio for the quarter stayed relatively high at 65.9%. Portfolio eliminations ran at a high 22.7% vs. buys of 9%. Berkshire is still swimming in cash, some $140 billion. Why? It sold out some 60% of its portfolio.

Pershing Square continues to run a relatively high static ratio, near 60%; Berkshire, a 14% holding, was eliminated. Lowe's, a huge winner, is now a 22% position, up from 15.7%. I'm impressed. Bill Ackman added to positions in Starbucks, Hilton International, Howard Hughes and Lowe's, a gutsy macro call on a reviving economic setting. I like the way Ackman runs money. The portfolio is conceptually coherent and aggressively concentrated in several one-off kind of stocks. The right way to go to the moon.

Walt Disney is popping up more often. A post-COVID-19 play is top position in Third Point, edging out Amazon. Baxter International was numero uno, now cut back from 16% of the list to a 4.7% position. This is a less defensive portfolio but not tech laden and doesn't make a strong statement—pro-recovery, but maybe not enough.

The Duquesne Family Office portfolio looks like mine with Microsoft numero uno, followed by Amazon. JPMorgan Chase, 4.6% of the portfolio, still leaves me cold. Static ratio is low at 10%, but this list looks like it fully captured the second quarter's zippy recovery.

When I step back from these portfolios, my feeling is that many high-intensity players don't believe in a more zippy market led by tech and internet houses. Almost all missed Apple and coulda had more Amazon. Facebook is light, and not enough Microsoft anywhere.

Hardly anyone is carrying large-capitalization energy plays, or drug houses, a good call, but why allergic to oil-service stocks like Halliburton, which bot-

Custodial vs. High-Intensity Money Managers

tomed at $4.25 and now ticks at $16? Likewise, Freeport-McMoRan more than doubled from its March low under $6. Non-durables stocks like Coca-Cola and Proctor & Gamble did rally but not eye-catching.

Overall, I'm surprised that so few money managers pushed their chips into the pot, post March's recovery. Consider, the NASDAQ-100 Index powered to a 40% gain for the quarter. Incidentally, these houses should be rated against NASDAQ, not the S&P 500. Simply, they mainly run compressed portfolios with stocks of above-average volatility. I'm surprised limited partners ignore this issue. During 2020, Tiger Global Management persisted in their construct of internet and e-commerce paper, maintaining a high static ratio of 62%, only exceeded by Berkshire Hathaway's stay-put portfolio of bank stocks and Apple. No Apple at Tiger.

Meanwhile Coatue, an $8 billion asset house, showed 100% turnover, a zero-static ratio, selling 40% of assets and buying 44%. Netflix was numero uno at 8.4%, a big beneficiary of stay-at-home viewing during the country's shut-in modality. When does this end?

What caught my eye at Renaissance Technologies is the portfolio was a pure distillation of a construct in noncyclical stocks like Bristol Myers Squibb and ending with Humana. This math-based house mainly focused on pharmaceuticals, but algorithms don't always work. The market got busy, second quarter of 2020, discounting broad-based cyclical resurgence. Renaissance missed out.

Conagra Brands was a 44% position in Java Partners, also supporting a zero-static ratio, but under a billion in assets. Depreciation was $411 million in the March 2020 quarter. Is this money management or sheer gunslinging?

Appaloosa lost around 17% of its asset value in the March quarter and continues with asset churning at a zero-static ratio. You're buying NASDAQ-100 Index herein. Top four positions account for 52% of the portfolio—Amazon, Alibaba, Alphabet and Facebook. New faces account for 43% of assets. I think all of us could do better sitting in our armchairs or solely buying the NASDAQ-100.

Icahn's portfolio always has kept to a high static ratio, at 68%, higher than Buffett's list. Market depreciation was over 30%. This is normally a special-situation portfolio, energy heavy, with Occidental Petroleum and Cheniere Energy.

Train to Outslug the Market

I don't get it. What's the theme, Carl? Commodity recovery coming? Occidental topped out at $54, leveraging itself for an untimely acquisition, now trading in mid-teens.

Greenlight Capital lost nearly half its invested capital in the March 2020 quarter. Top three positions, half its capital, rested in properties I've never heard of: Green Brick Partners, Brighthouse Financial and AerCap Holdings. From its February high, Green Brick was cut in half but has come back some. Paulson had a horrific quarter, too, down nearly 45%. There's a gold play here now with 25% of assets therein. It's working. If I had more guts, I'd short gold here. The gold bugs rest too complacently.

Finally, we get to Pershing Square Capital Management, a $6.5 billion house that held its own in the March quarter, an outstanding report bar none. Short selling? Some 60% in cash was reinvested and its static ratio was at a low 10%. Pershing held 22% of Howard Hughes, tied to land development. Lowe's, Pershing's major position at 16% of assets, sits as a great recovery spec tied to the home-improvement sector, and a play on a turnover in the existing housing-stock inventory. I missed this good bet. Hilton Worldwide Holdings, a pure spec on recovery in hotel occupancy and revenue per room, for me discounts half the recovery in store next two years.

Wannabe billionaires need to grind it out stock picking, quarter by quarter. But centurion billionaires like Bill Gates, Jeff Bezos, Mark Zuckerberg and Jack Ma made it through the capitalized value of their companies, not net-asset value accretion. If you measured net worth by what jingles in your pocket, book value, you'd have to reduce such owner net worth, anywhere up to 80%. Their unrealized gains would be taxed by a winning Democrat's presidency.

Berkshire, over five years, underperformed both the S&P 500 Index and a peer group of insurance properties. The peer group is irrelevant because Berkshire is much more than Geico and its reinsurance holdings. Underperforming by 13% is a meaningful shortfall, but ignored by shareholders, so far.

Anyone who missed big tech in the June quarter should be called on the carpet for an explanation…and then terminated.

Custodial vs. High-Intensity Money Managers

BERKSHIRE'S UNDERPERFORMANCE

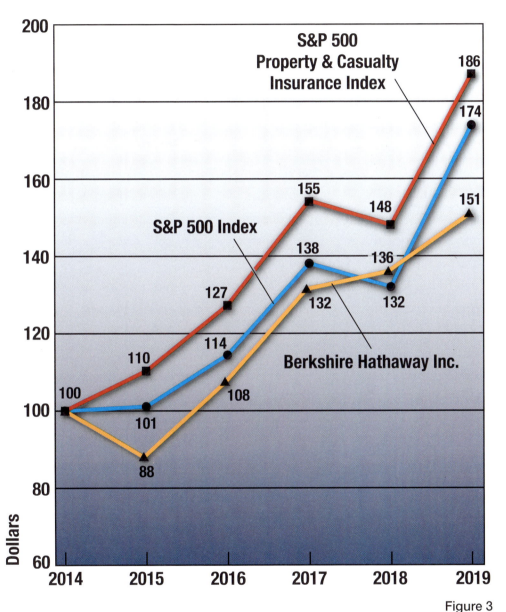

Figure 3
Source: Berkshire Hathaway 2019, Form 10-K

Does Buffett Deserve His Market Premium?

Next couple of years, I'd expect Berkshire Hathaway's 20% premium over asset value to melt away. What could make me wrong? Outperforming the S&P 500 Index would be a starter, along with recovery in operating earnings for insurance properties and owned industrials like Precision Castparts, the BNSF Railway Company and Lubrizol.

Add in a recovery for banks like Wells Fargo and Bank of America. The Apple position truly is a home run, now dwarfing all other positions at $112 billion. On Berkshire's equity base, over $400 billion, Apple sits at 25% and is half the portfolio's asset value.

Berkshire Hathaway's Five Top Holdings
(in billions)

	June 30, 2020	Yearend 2019
Apple	112.0	73.7
Bank of America	27.0	33.4
The Coca-Cola Company	19.5	22.1
American Express	15.2	18.9
Wells Fargo (1)	10.0	18.6

(1) Sold out

Does Buffett Deserve His Market Premium?

Everyone's entitled to one or two portfolio luxuries, but Buffett has carried such a concept to extremes with great courage. I can rationalize outsized Apple, alone, a surrogate to technology's sector weighting in the S&P 500 Index. Buffett's pretty naked therein.

Portfolio concentration pretty much rivals a high-intensity hedge fund operator like Bill Ackman at Pershing Square, but this is a $6.5 billion house. Even he carried a position in Berkshire. His pick of Lowe's, a winner, is actually a Buffett-kinda-value play. Pershing's 22% holding in Howard Hughes was one of a couple of real estate cyclical-recovery specs. Mine are Halliburton and Freeport-McMoRan. Betting on the end of deflation in our system next 12 months could be wishful thinking, but I'm all in, fingers crossed.

Berkshire's huge overconcentration in the financial sector is difficult for me to rationalize today. It happened over decades and historically was a great play in a sector with a low price-earnings ratio. August of 2020, oversized financial holdings at $52 billion became overshadowed by Apple. The bruising from Wells Fargo and Bank of America, over $15 billion, was sizable.

Berkshire's market capitalization tots up to roughly $500 billion. Frame of reference, Facebook's at $675 billion, buoyant but considered problematic. Conceptually, anyone can buy Apple and a few bank stocks, say JPMorgan Chase and Citigroup, thereby eliminating the "Buffett premium." Why not? His five top holdings at $185 billion comprise the heart of his portfolio assets.

Had Buffett gone off the "deep end"? Maybe yes, maybe no, but for sure I don't like his major holdings, excepting Apple. Don't mark him down for having owned airlines, IBM, even Exxon Mobil in past years. Everyone's entitled to some bad picks. Warren did miss great five-year plays in internet and e-commerce paper—namely Facebook, Alphabet, Amazon, Alibaba and Microsoft.

Obviously, such paper rested outside Buffett's comfort zone of security analysis. Why pay a huge premium for a property that isn't analyzable using traditional security analysis? Apple was his perfect pick. You could juggle with its metrics and if you liked the product offerings, Apple's price-earnings ratio was comparable with the market, within the zone of 15 to 18 times forward

Train to Outslug the Market

12-month numbers. After all the hype, Amazon remains unanalyzable. Forty-two analysts bless it, maybe one nay and two neutrals.

Approximately half of Berkshire's net worth rests in publicly traded stocks, but Buffett never discusses his picks, covering their fundamentals, the rationale for bank stocks today and expectations for growth at Apple. Investors coast along for the ride, elongated into years. The turnover ratio for the portfolio (the static ratio) is as low as it gets in the world of money managers. Static ratios for operators like Carl Icahn can run high, too, over 50%, but Buffett's can be 80%, at least 60%, consistently.

When I focused on Berkshire's wholly-owned operating companies, I was surprised to find how vulnerable to COVID-19 stood Precision Castparts, Lubrizol, even the consumer sector and BNSF. Insurance properties' investment income account hangs in while losses in reinsurance stay sizable. Geico's underwriting profitability is peaking as givebacks are due to policyholders who aren't driving so much these days.

The write-down in goodwill, over $10 billion in Precision Castparts, surprised me. This is a very high-quality aerospace industrial. There's still $71 billion in goodwill left on the balance sheet from past acquisitions, a big number. Buffett's dream of prolific franchises in operating entities seems temporarily impaired. Analytically, I'd put a mid-teens multiplier on earnings of operating companies, inclusive of BNSF and Lubrizol. Paying sizable control premiums on deals can end up costing you long term.

Net, net, Berkshire is an operating conglomerate of industrials, retailing, energy, insurance underwriting and money management. Historically, conglomerate properties sell below market valuation. If relative asset value accretion from money management still proves elusive, Berkshire will remain an underperforming piece of paper, probably losing its 20% premium over net asset value.

Nothing is forever, but Warren has come close these past 60 years. Change in configuration of its market assets is meaningful. Over 25% of net worth now rests in the Apple position, about double the $50 billion in banks and American Express. Sizable entities in manufacturing stand victimized by COVID-19's hailstorm. Not the time for railroads like BNSF, Precision Castparts and oil-related Lubrizol. Precision Castparts was a $37 billion acquisition in 2016.

I applaud Buffett for singling out American Express and Coca-Cola early on, when Wall Street was asleep on the potency of their franchises, five decades ago.

Sosnoff's Five Largest Holdings
(August 2020)

Facebook	10.9%
Alibaba	10.0%
Microsoft	8.6%
Amazon	7.7%
Freeport-McMoRan	6.8%

Some comparisons:

I've got 44% of assets in five stocks. Fairly aggressive, unhedged money management, but I don't report results to anyone nor file 13Fs quarterly. I'm sole honcho. Microsoft gave me a double past 12 months. Initial position under 5%.

Conceptually, I loathe bank stocks. They use tons of leverage, which periodically gets them in deep trouble, like 2008–2009. Now, they've gotten cheap— little premium over book value, excepting JPMorgan Chase. Banks are selling near 10 to 12 times average mid-cycle earnings power. This seems a fair entry point, even with minimal interest rates still an earnings depressant. Why can't we see negative interest rates in a depressed business-cycle setting going on and on? Look at Europe. I'm agnostic.

5

How $5 Stocks Turn into $10 Stocks (Then More)

My experience with $5 to $10 paper is you need half a dozen because some land in Tap City while others rumble up to $25 in a year or less. For example, during the panic in oil over OPEC's stupidity, Halliburton plunged from $25 at yearend 2019 to $5 in just three months. By midyear it recovered to $14. Schlumberger, previously considered a polite institutional stock, dropped from $44 to $12, over 70%. Management finally cut its dividend from $2 to 50 cents, recognizing reality with current earnings power possibly of a buck a share or less.

At their bottom, both Halliburton and Schlumberger sold no more than 12 times current depressed earnings power. My take on the S&P 500 Index was it ticked at 18 times normalized earnings. So, clearly pricey barring a solid recovery from the shut-in ambiance of depressed earnings power, spring of 2020.

What's remarkable on big bounces for both Halliburton and Schlumberger is if you caught Halliburton's March bottom of $4.61, you'd have tripled your money in four months. Late July, Halliburton traded in size over $14. The recovery for Schlumberger was less remarkable, a lousy 50%.

I wish I could say that I caught the bottom in Halliburton, but I didn't. My average cost was $7 and change. I passed on Schlumberger because I believed it was an overrated company. Before I cottoned to Halliburton, I performed some security analysis. This was not a seat-of-your-pants kind of play. You look for operating earnings power before charge-offs.

First, consider the under-$10 universe, spring 2020. I surveyed it broad picture rather than sharp-penciled. The list embraced Ford Motor, General

How $5 Stocks Turn into $10 Stocks (Then More)

HALLIBURTON'S UNDULATIONS

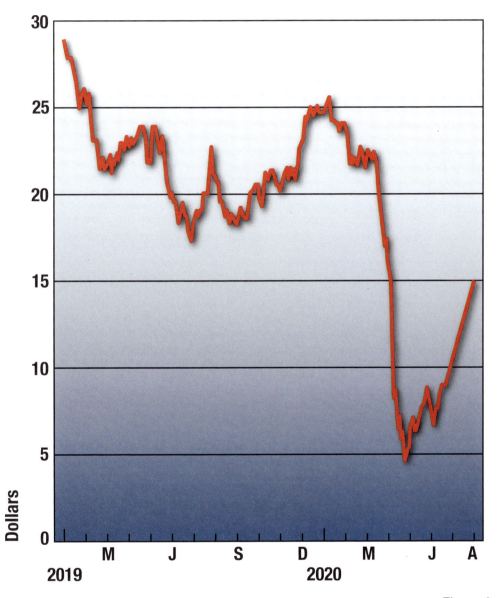

Figure 4
Source: Bloomberg (chart reproduction)

Electric, Alcoa, U.S. Steel, Halliburton, Macy's and Energy Transfer Partners, an MLP yielding 16%. Then, throw in Teva Pharmaceutical Industries, which had slid down from a 12-month high of $15.72 to $6. Finally, I took a good look at Freeport-McMoRan.

Early exclusions were easy to make. Any company that I thought might face bankruptcy next 12 months, I eliminated. Then, I excluded properties where I thought economic recovery was over 12 months out. Exclusions were easy. They embraced Ford Motor, U.S. Steel and Macy's. On General Electric I felt the outlook for aerospace was troublesome because of Boeing's disasters, their order book waxing thinner and thinner.

Finally, I excluded Alcoa because I didn't care for deep involvement in the materials sector. Here my GDP forecast, which was muted, came into play. I did buy Freeport because I believed it had balance-sheet strength to weather deeply depressed quotes for copper.

Halliburton ended up my biggest recovery spec because management showed serious recognition of the deep-down cycle for oil drilling and field servicing. There was one last exercise in security analysis. I had to deal with the issue of an elongated down cycle. Could the company's balance sheet carry them through?

All this goes back to what I learned about balance-sheet analysis from Mike Milken. Here, the MAD ratio is applied to the property in question. This test invokes the market value of the stock in question to its debt outstanding. **What you want to see is no more than a one-to-one ratio, that the market value of the company at least equals the market value of balance-sheet debt.** This comfortable ratio suggests the harried company can raise more debt financing if called upon because of operating losses.

A year ago, Halliburton's ratio was a comfortable 2.5 to 1. But when the stock traded down to five bucks, the MAD ratio stood at one to one. This was my cutoff point, why I wouldn't buy the stock at $5. Then it rallied to $7 and I stepped in. A comparable analysis was made for Freeport-McMoRan. They could soldier through the worst scenario I could postulate, near bankruptcy.

How $5 Stocks Turn into $10 Stocks (Then More)

Nothing's easy. Daily price fluctuations of 10% draw gut-wrenching attention. Such goods are playthings of market traders. For all I knew, the ratio of stock valuation of Halliburton to an index of cyclical stocks could touch off a buy signal for a bunch of computer nerds monitoring their algorithms, minute-by-minute.

My final pick was Energy Transfer Partners, which touched down at $3.75 from a high of $15.42. Current yield, spring '20, with the stock at $7.30, was 16%. I'm assuming yield could be halved if distributable cash flow isn't covered by operating revenues. Here I'm a captive of my apperceptive mass on energy master-limited partnerships.

This was an energy industry subsector that the major oil companies discarded because it wasn't big enough to matter to them. A bunch of high-risk operators stepped in with leveraged balance sheets and built out oil and LPG pipelines and storage facilities. Now, they've cut back expansion plans and have learned to keep shareholder distributions within their distributable cash flow. Hell-bent-for-leather exuberance is history. Hopefully they'd weather through low but not washed-out energy quotes.

Ironically, I felt more comfortable with my handful of ragamuffins than I did with holdings in Amazon, Facebook, Microsoft and Alibaba. Who am I to pontificate what's the proper price-earnings ratio for such market leaders? I can't project comfortably their earnings power next three years. They may be super risky, selling at huge multiples of operating cash flow and unpredictable earnings power.

Normally, a $1,000 stock contains more motive force than a $5 piece of paper, but not in today's setting. Actually, it became a management conceit never to split your stock. It started with Warren Buffett decades ago, and seems to say, "Let's drop our pants and measure tools."

Ultimate risk is embedded in all our financial markets, inclusive of equities, oil, junk bonds, currency and interest-rate futures. Volatility is our way of life. Who woulda thought that oil futures could trade below zero, with money market rates near zero and junk bonds fluctuating 5% overnight? I remember Treasuries yielding 15%, not next to zero today. Stocks like Ford Motor, General Electric and Macy's trade closer to $5 than $10 because of shaky capital structures and unchartable fundamentals which adumbrate ultimate risk.

I can't project the world's steel demand, so U.S. Steel is off my list. So is Alcoa, but it bounced up, too. Lest we forget Microsoft, a trillion-dollar piece of paper doubled past 12 months and sells at 1.8 times the market's multiplier. No sleepless nights incurred. I expect Microsoft to appreciate 2%, monthly, next couple of years. It's definable and can be modeled confidently.

Consider: Halliburton, past January, ticked at $25. Yes, 25 bucks, and then oil futures collapsed. If oil finds its way again, above $40 a barrel, Halliburton could break out and double from its 10 bucks level. Demand for generic drugs has reasserted itself.

There're a bunch of MLP stocks that trade in the mid-teens on high payouts of distributable cash-flow yields that range into double digits. Enterprise Products Partners is the quality piece of paper. I own a $7 number, Energy Transfer, when the yield is unmentionably higher but not so secure. ET has doubled from its $3.75 low. These midstream operators need to see steady throughput for oil and gas in their pipeline constructs, the pivotal variable here.

There's another class of wasted stocks that cover big-capitalization multi-nationals. I've much respect for the achievements of Walt Disney, American Express, even JPMorgan Chase, which traded 40% below yearend 2019 highs. The investment issue was determination of how soon earnings power reasserted itself in a post-coronavirus world setting. Secular properties like Biogen, Netflix and Coca-Cola left me cold because of their high premium relative to the market. Mid-2020, financials as post-COVID-19 comeback prospects stopped rallying.

Deeply imbedded for all of us is the concept that stocks can sell anywhere, too high or too low. When there's a good reason to pull the trigger, a buy or sell, do it.

What to Do if Unafraid

The crossover from passive investor to Wall Street operator takes an emotional commitment to being right as well as having brass hubris. You can't play the cowardly lion. It's "John Waynesville" or bite the dust. Decades ago, when I asked Rupert Murdoch if he would sell me a big block of News Corporation stock when it was trading at a single digit in Australia, he looked at me as if I were totally insane. "I'm never going below arithmetic control," he said in his flat, matter-of-fact Australian accent.

The capacity of a great operator to continually surprise his shareholders is the biggest thrill I get out of managing money. By the millennium, News Corp. had become a major player in film production (Fox) as well as satellite and television broadcasting. Its market capitalization zoomed to over $40 billion, then $80 billion. Rupert's bold entry into satellite broadcasting (Sky Group) was a home run.

The New York Times Company now is zippy, thanks to internet subscriptions to the paper. But it was in business for 150 years and its market capitalization only measured up to $7 billion. Great newspapermen, mediocre businessmen.

Sam Walton founded Walmart and took shareholders to the moon as well as his family. Early on, Walton divided his equity into equal parts for family members who now are worth $40 billion, apiece.

I bought American Express at the same time (1964) as Buffett, who's held on, doggedly. After a couple of years, I took my profits. Same for Geico, which traded down to near receivership. A few years later, I banged it out at 10 bucks while Buffett made it the cornerstone of his insurance commitment, inclusive of General Reinsurance.

Aside from frugality and courage as expressed by Buffett, Loews' Larry Tisch, Sam Walton as well as operators like Sam Zell, Charles Schwab, Carl Icahn and Michael Milken all possessed the intensity of singlemindedness and staying power. Add Rupert Murdoch and Ted Turner. I remember Mike Milken lugging around two lawyer satchels filled with deal papers. Michael frequently programmed two or even three breakfasts in one morning when he came back to New York.

Nobody can dodge market volatility. One day in May 2020 I watched the energy sector, particularly oil service stocks like Halliburton and Schlumberger, sink 10% intraday. Same goes for bank stocks like Citigroup, even JPMorgan Chase and materials issues like Freeport-McMoRan, U.S. Steel and Alcoa. The market was busy that day burying stocks tied to a deflationary setting of near-zero interest rates. Oil futures traded near zero, down from $40 a barrel not many months ago.

Instead of panicking, I looked at this negative setting and said to myself it's not the end of the trajectory of the world. Bank stocks like Citigroup and JPMorgan Chase had traded down close to book value from premiums as high as 50%. Exxon Mobil was yielding 7.8% and I knew management would rather slit their throats than radically reduce their cash payout. Halliburton had traded down from a high of $29 to five bucks, but management was doggedly reducing headcount and capital spending. I didn't buy Exxon Mobil because I'm prejudiced against many big-capitalization properties. It was a big mistake. The stock bottomed at $32 and a month later traded at $50.

And yet, you can use a broad analytical brush rather than a sharp-penciled analysis of an unfolding event.

Call this analysis "at the margin." New facts emerge, sometimes unexpected, overnight. Corporations miss on earnings expectations, the headman dies in a plane crash, an anticipated phase-three testing of a dementia drug proves disappointing. The stocks involved drop 10%, overnight. Sometimes more. Normally,

What to Do if Unafraid

I don't overreact immediately to news at the margin, but on Boeing's 737 MAX crashing, I sold out my position because I extrapolated this was a fundamental change in prospects. It was the right decision, Boeing's stock ranging down from $430 to below $100 over a 12-month period. The stock then doubled over a couple of months from the market's low in March 2020. I missed the recovery because I couldn't build a credible-income statement on future-years' earnings power. Damaged goods.

Boeing had turned into a gut play. You had to believe they had sufficient borrowing power to endure even the demise of the 737 as a profit center. I couldn't make this leap of faith so I wasn't a player and had no regrets.

I assume most everyone is time-limited and can't bring to the table intensive financial analysis that reviews all variables in a situation. However, on macro events like a market panic touched off by a 9/11 happening, a bank's failure, Russia reneging on its Treasury notes, Paul Volcker raising interest rates to 15% to stem inflation, the individual investor's point of view is as good as any pundit's, even the chairman of the Federal Reserve Board or the head of the International Monetary Fund. They rarely get it right, especially overnight or even for months.

You don't play the cowardly lion, but step in and buy the NASDAQ-100 or even futures on the S&P 500 Index. **Whatever market sectors are hardest hit, whether it be technology, financials or industrials, you buy or add to the biggest-capitalization stocks, because if you're wrong you can bang 'em out in a matter of minutes, trading electronically.**

The only way I know of developing a strong individualistic point of view on where the country is headed and its long-term issues that impinge on GDP growth, interest rates and inflation is to study historical charts covering our entire postwar history. Same goes for financial markets that track cycles of growth and recession.

The stock market always overreacts to change at the margin. It becomes overvalued or undervalued based on expectations of its players, who are never right for very long. The Street's music sheets lean toward overoptimism. None of the pundits ever comes out with a call that the market is clearly overvalued

Train to Outslug the Market

and investors should lighten up a lot.

Anyone with serious money to invest should subscribe to a chart service covering our economy and financial markets. Trends in taxation, employment, federal spending and Federal Reserve Board policy emphasis are critical variables for investing. Almost all pronouncements quarterly from our government deal only with the current quarter compared with year-ago numbers. Financial publications like the Wall Street Journal rarely add perspective, publishing comparative results going back five or 10 years on the deficit, GDP growth, inflation, the trade balance, federal spending and unemployment by sectors.

Here's a chart that I've found invaluable in understanding long-term dynamics of the country and financial markets' valuation dating back to early postwar years:

With the market selling at the least 18 times normalized earnings in mid-2020, historically it's at full valuation. The price-earnings ratio here is related to the interest-rate setting. When interest rates are low, below 4%, valuation is elevated. The reason for a low price-earnings ratio with interest rates near zero was the country remained in its Great Depression setting during the thirties. No earnings story.

High interest rates for bonds impact valuation. At 5% or higher, the earnings multiple can sink below teens level to remain competitive with bond yields. Anyone forecasting the market has to rationalize his projections based on where he sees interest rates and the course of inflation in the country.

After the market's 2020 retracement, it still sold at a huge premium over book value. Call it 1.8 times its net assets, while yielding 2%. If the coronavirus isn't contained with vaccinations, look out below. A market at book value, 10 times apparent earnings and yielding 5% would take us back to around 1,000 on the S&P 500. Before dismissing this scenario, consider it took place in the financial meltdown of 2008–2009. Same goes for 1982 when Paul Volcker took Treasury rates up to 15% to rid the country of its inflationary expectations at 7% to 8% per annum.

Consider: Energy paper like Schlumberger, Exxon Mobil and Halliburton swing 10% or more intraday, and traded 50% or more below their highs. Same

What to Do if Unafraid

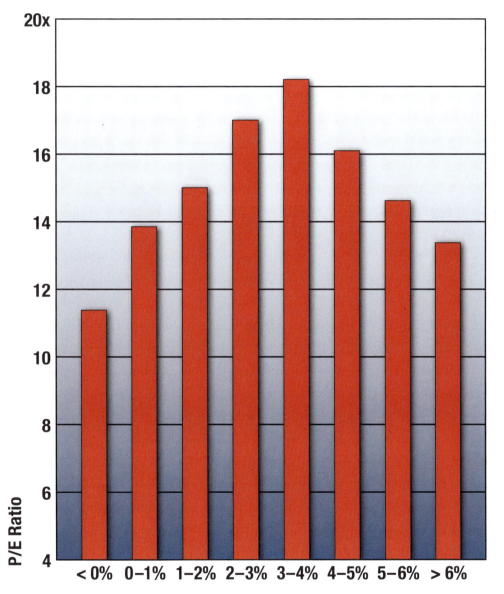

Figure 5

Source: Thomson Reuters & Morgan Stanley

Train to Outslug the Market

goes for banks like Citigroup, even JPMorgan Chase. For gaming casinos like Wynn Resorts, it's repeatedly a 10% variance along with aerospace names like Boeing and Spirit AeroSystems Holdings.

By comparison, tech and e-trade stocks like Amazon, Alibaba, Microsoft, even Apple seemed like polite paper, half as volatile as the market or less. There's a rationale for such variance. Major tech houses carry ample balance-sheet strength, sizable free-cash flow and don't pay dividends. They can outlast even a deep recession without even a cutback in R&D spending.

No other sector of the market sports unassailable balance-sheet strength. Pharmaceuticals come close, but dividends across the industrial sector are suspect. Same goes for energy. Autos and aerospace will need sizable infusions of federal capital while a default crisis in the bond sector would need FRB attention.

In technology, I'm willing to look across the valley of 2020–2021. My assumptions aren't particularly rosy, expecting it takes all of 2020 for the country to stamp out most COVID-19 cases. The fourth quarter could mark the nadir in earnings losses for large and small businesses. Consumer spending and single-family housing bottoms out, and auto sales recover at a moderate pace.

Present money managers, maybe those in their late forties, did experience the tech bubble of 2000–2001, but on Black Monday, October of 1987, they were just learning long division in grade school. How many of us experienced the horrendous real-estate recession of 1973–1974? Prime co-ops went for under $100,000 in the Big Apple, and builders watched equity in Fifth Avenue office space dwindle to petty cash, billions below book value.

My chart on long-term oil futures, a 2015 construct, then put them at a $72 peak in 2020 from $52 in 2015. So much for long-term charting. Everyone missed how geopolitics can lead economics. With play money, I just bought a couple of MLPs, Enterprise Products Partners and Williams Companies. They yield over 8%.

The sole time oil futures traded under $20 a barrel was 2002. Two years later, futures ticked at $40, then peaked at over $140 in 2009. Don't ask me why.

What to Do if Unafraid

Six years ago, Microsoft sold at a 10% discount to the S&P 500. God knows why! Yearend 1972 the market traded at 18 times earnings, where we were months ago.

In 1972, heady valuations failed to hold up. A decade later, Polaroid, Xerox, Avon Products and Eastman Kodak turned into goat meat. Schlumberger sold at 57 times earnings then and Sears, Roebuck at a 29 multiplier. These were once proud managements, now humbled, scrambling to endure vicious changes in their businesses from upstart competitors like Walmart. Without a sense of valuation for growth and value plays, prospective investors should probe the depth of a market with index funds—growth, value and NASDAQ.

Leave the COVID-19 longevity aside. Buying into a strong market is safer than being premature. Let the sun come up like a red rubber ball. My shopping list, spring of 2020, covered Walt Disney, Apple, Citigroup plus more Facebook and Alibaba. Ragamuffins like Freeport-McMoRan and Halliburton, looking-over-the-valley stocks, got my money because I believed they had the wherewithal to ride out deep recession. **In short, the hardest things to do make you the most money, but, start with a probe.**

Three months later, these probes and add-ons surged at least 50%, Halliburton doubled, Freeport-McMoRan too.

Easy Sell-Down to Your Sleeping Level

The only sound advice ever given on market panics came from Bernard Baruch. Some poor devil thrust his portfolio (written on a scrap of paper) in Bernie's face and asked what he should do. Baruch swiped away the paper without a look and told him, "Sell down to your sleeping level."

My experience in free-falling markets when big-capitalization stocks do drop 5% to 10% intraday goes back to the sixties during the Cuban Missile Crisis. Then President Kennedy's face-off with Roger Blough, headman at U.S. Steel, queered the market. Blough had tacked on a steel price bump at a time when JFK was trying to accelerate GDP growth and quiet inflation.

Those days, the market's printout was on an electromechanical tape that stuttered noisily across your desk. When the Russian freighter carrying more missiles to Cuba was hauled to by our Coast Guard, the tape was running five hours late. I had put my buy orders on a slip of paper, then into a pneumatic tube and hoped for the best. Today, you get instant gratification trading electronically.

Normally, I'm a fully invested bull in definable properties that I can model at least a year out, hopefully longer. Call me a disciplined player, pretty focused on big-capitalization growth stocks. Today, it's Amazon, Facebook, Alibaba and Microsoft. I no longer own banks because of the rapidly flattened yield curve. Hate energy and turn up my nose on industrials and materials paper.

Spring of 2020, I saw enormous intraday price swings on iconic properties like Exxon Mobil, Halliburton, Citigroup, JPMorgan Chase, Adobe, General

Motors, even DuPont and Dow Chemical. I'm talking about moves of 10% to 15%. There's Schlumberger in free-fall yielding 14%, but not fully covered by cash flow. It got sharply reduced. Don't miss Occidental Petroleum, down 40%, yielding 21% but not for long. The dividend was finally eliminated. Warren Buffett's portfolio was a train wreck in the making with 40% resting in banks and American Express. I saw JPMorgan down 15% intraday. But, hold on. On May 18, these same sinkers reversed themselves. Halliburton, alone, rose 15%. The market decided to look over the valley and discount recovery, that a COVID-19 vaccine was possibly no more than six months away.

Only portfolio structure, not stock picking, can save you in a wildly swinging market. Traditional wealth managers like JPMorgan, with trillions in assets, run portfolios pretty close to a 60-40 ratio of equities to fixed income assets. They've underperformed past couple of years, largely missing big movers in the NASDAQ-100 Index, but at least they won't bury clients in a bear market, particularly with 10-year Treasuries headed to a zero yield.

There's an eerie silence pervading the Street on what's the proper price-earnings ratio for the market, mid-2020. Nobody blanches at current valuation of 18 times normalized earnings. Actually, there's some historical validation for an 18-times multiplier when interest rates rest under 2% in a minimal inflationary setting.

But periods of calm are few and far between. Never last much more than a year or so. Normally, there's a push-pull. When interest rates are low, corporate earnings turn spotty. For example, materials properties like U.S. Steel and Alcoa have lost more than two-thirds of valuation over 12 months. With a leveraged balance sheet, I'm not sure U.S Steel is a survivor.

Let's wrestle with the issue of what's the proper price-earnings ratio for this market in our world, dodging the pandemic. I threw up my hands on putting a number on 2021's corporate earnings. My feel was the numbers will disappoint, covering every industry sector of the S&P 500 Index, including prime-growth stocks like Microsoft and Alphabet. I proved wrong on supergrowth stocks. They held their own, Facebook actually making new highs. I sleep better at a

Train to Outslug the Market

50/50 debt-equity ratio.

So...the puzzle is, can 2021 be a comeback setting for corporate earnings? I'll be generous and put up a number of $170 a share. But I can't be too generous on the valuation multiplier for the market. I'm at 15 times earnings. Even if all's right with the world, our market isn't worth more than 2,500, but it sells at 2,950. Somebody's extrapolating higher earnings than my number.

If the world doesn't get its hands around the coronavirus soon, all bets are off the table. Earnings would collapse at least 20% for even prime growthies. Face the facts, our market still sells near two times book value. Decades back, it took over 15 years for the market to break through its valuation multiplier of 15 times earnings. Do you remember 1987's Black Monday? The market dropped 22%. Traders at Salomon Brothers wouldn't pick up their phones, afraid to make block bids even for their best clients.

But Black Monday shouldn't have been so great a shock. After all, the market had topped out a month earlier, and interest rates surged over 7%. Deal proliferation filled the air out Mike Milken's way in Beverly Hills. The moronic fad of portfolio insurance had captured institutional investors. I was busy setting up a $1 billion line of credit to do a deal. My loan rate was 7.5% with a 1% standby fee for the bank syndicate. I didn't even blink at such rate insanity.

If it's too hard to build an earnings model for the coming 12 months, sell down to a 50% invested structure. It's that simple. Put the other 50% in high-yield bonds if yielding over 5% with five-year duration. Short of a deep recession, they're money good.

Just in case you're feeling complacent about your technology holdings, reference this chart on the NASDAQ Composite Index. Time period is the prelude to the technology bubble in 2000 and its aftermath. From 1998 to 2000 the index soared from 1,500 to over 5,000. The denouement was complete, even symmetrical retracement. NASDAQ bottomed near 1,000 early in 2002. Mid-2020, this index ticked at 10,000.

Easy Sell-Down to Your Sleeping Level

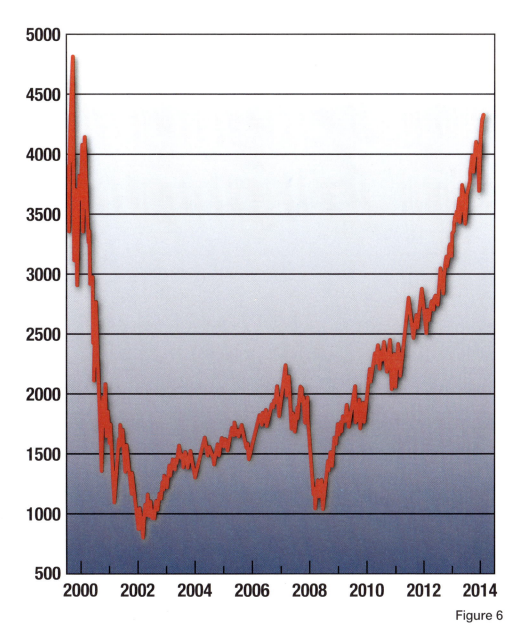

Figure 6
Source: Bloomberg (chart reproduction)

Train to Outslug the Market

Obviously, a lot happened. The next bear market would witness the crushing of trillion-dollar capitalizations like Amazon, Microsoft and Apple as well as Alibaba, Alphabet and Facebook. Most everyone shies away from NASDAQ because of inherent volatility, but during the COVID-19 malaise, this index outperformed the S&P 500 Index and turned positive by mid-2020.

The bank industry chart turned into Niagara Falls in the financial meltdown of 2008–2009. From the peak of 120, the KBW Bank Index plummeted to 20, over a 12-month period.

As for terming art an emotional asset, consider the panic in bank stocks during the financial meltdown of 2008–2009. This index dropped from 120 to 20. Now that's an emotional asset, a bank stock in disarray.

Easy Sell-Down to Your Sleeping Level

KBW BANK INDEX

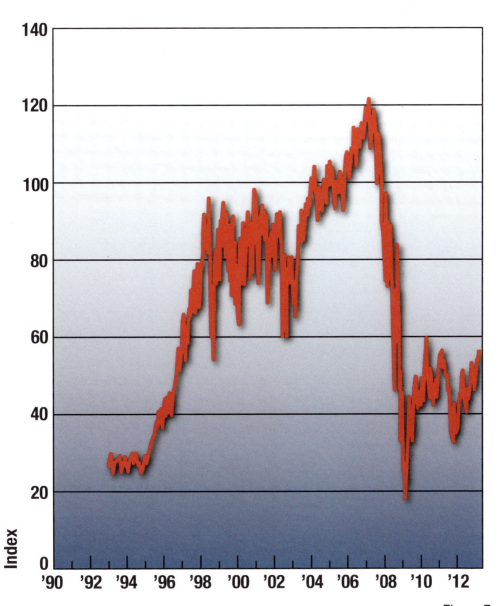

Figure 7

Source: Bloomberg (chart reproduction)

Emotional Assets Put Away Venture Capital Returns

In thought-controlled China, some of the world's best contemporary art is being produced. The authorities don't know what to make of it so they don't clamp down. The roots of German neo-expressionism date back to Nazi Germany's atrocities; the younger generation's reactions, remembrances and sympathies for those annihilated were deeply expressed.

They say high net-worth individuals carry 10% of their net worth in art and sundry collectibles. Consider, collectibles have outperformed government bonds, gold and T-bills, up 6.4% in nominal terms, 2.4% in real returns for over 100 years.

At some point in my life as a collector of contemporary art, the locus of my net worth moved sharply from financial assets and real estate to art. I didn't plan it that way and wasn't even aware of this phenomenon until Sotheby's performed an evaluation of our collection, based on recent sales of comparable works at auction.

I started collecting in my early twenties, the mid-fifties, when the New York School of abstract expressionism made New York the art capital of the world. My average expenditure was $300 for a work. Nobody but David Rockefeller and Peggy Guggenheim then possessed serious money allocated to art. I bought work from my friends in Woodstock, artists without galleries, paying for my picks $25, monthly. My salary as a copy editor then was 100 bucks, weekly, and when I made my way down to Wall Street, they started me at 100 bucks, too, but paid for my MBA tuition at New York University, if I got Bs or better.

I remember being unable to cough up $1,200 for a Mark Rothko painting offered me by Betty Parsons in 1954. Meanwhile, Sam Kootz, who showed Picasso and Soulages, took me under his wing and tutored me. By the mid-sixties, I could afford Soulages then going for $30,000, now $8 million.

Even Jackson Pollock's work, which nobody understood but everybody was intrigued by, went for $1,000, early fifties. Late fifties, Rothko's soft colorist work was offered at $7,000 to $8,000. David Rockefeller, who was tutored by the head of MoMA, bought them. David built a wondrous collection of abstract expressionist work which he showed in his corporate headquarters at One Chase Manhattan Plaza. Graciously, Rockefeller encouraged me to come up and take a look. I was a tenant then at One Chase. The receptionists would giggle over the work, which they found silly and inscrutable. Decades later, Rockefeller's building was found to be asbestos-ridden, but his art collection was worth more than the building itself.

I learned about collecting from dealers and friends like Arthur Goldberg and Steve Mazoh, but I could never do what Steve did when he was an active dealer. If he liked an artist's work, he'd buy 20 or 30 paintings and put them in storage for future sales. For better or worse, I was a collector, not a trader in art or a dealer. Yes, if I liked an artist, I'd buy five or 10 pieces of his work, but only for hanging on our walls. We bought a 17,000-square-foot manor house on the Hudson River and filled every inch of suitable wall space.

The charts and tables on historical trends for collectibles really don't do justice to the exponential price elevation for subsectors of the art market like abstract expressionism since the early fifties. What they do show is relatively minimal real returns from the year 1900 to 2012 of 2.4% and 6.4% in nominal terms. Prices dropped meaningfully during World Wars I and II. I remember reading stories of Rembrandts sold by fleeing refugees from Hitler, for $7,500.

Economists, mainly ignorant of the contemporary art market since 1950, term art an "emotional asset" as if it were some foolish category unrelated to real assets like Treasury bonds, equities and real estate. But the sideshow in contemporary art since 1950 puts rates of return for even venture capitalists as puny by comparison.

Growth stocks, already established and viable, do appreciate 100% or 200% over five years, a few over 1,000%, but nowhere near what sought-after paintings go for. These days, any mogul can step up and pay $50 million for a Picasso, even a Warhol, Richter, Jeff Koons or Jasper Johns, and feel secure because he thinks he's well advised and after all, a half-dozen others are raising their paddles at Sotheby's and Christie's evening auctions. Ken Griffin, founder of Citadel, coughed up over $100 million for a Basquiat canvas mid-2020. You're late, Ken.

I never bought an artwork that I thought would appreciate in value. Au contraire, I believed nobody would ever relieve me of my stupid picks. Invariably, the more difficult, even ugly and incomprehensible the piece, it tended to mellow in no more than 25 years. Impressionism in the 1860s, however, took 40 to 50 years to be deemed collectible rather than laughable and ugly.

Bernard Berenson, known affectionately as BB, had it right in his work *Italian Painters of the Renaissance* when he opined that unless you had an emotional reaction to what you were viewing head-on, pass it by. I've collected using that rule of personal reaction above all.

But you've got to see everything possible. Read biographies of artists as well as critical examinations. If there's a catalogue raisonné available, I'd buy it and view the development of an artist's oeuvre during his lifetime of productivity.

I remember a rainy Saturday morning in SoHo, downtown New York. My wife and I were in Ileana Sonnabend's gallery, where she was showing Georg Baselitz paintings. I pointed to a big canvas of a nude lying facedown in the sand. "You can have it for $27,000," Ileana said. "I hate that piece. If you do buy it, I'll ship it up to your apartment later today. I want it out of here." That's how I acquired *Frau Am Strand.*

Frau Am Strand, 1981, by Georg Baselitz.
© Georg Baselitz 2020.

As BB said, "Many see pictures without knowing what to look at." Same goes for stocks. Ileana was one of the world's great collectors of contemporary art, and after her death, her collection toured museums worldwide.

Perception in the financial world is comparable with art. I feel most secure in my picks when nobody has said much about them that's constructive, or has even been negative. As for art, view the work of many artists, go to gallery shows or even walk up seven flights of stairs to see what's happening in their lofts. It helps if there's an elevator in the building.

9

The Value Investor's Dilemma (Can't X-Out Growth)

Decades ago, my countess and I took breakfast in the General Motors cafeteria on the second floor of the GM Building on 59th Street and Fifth Avenue. It was one of those quietly delicious insider moves New Yorkers practice. Never use the Triborough Bridge even when the toll-free Willis Avenue span is backed up. Don't call Sixth Avenue by its new name, Avenue of the Americas. That's for tourists.

The GM Building was always premium space. You paid plenty for the view of Central Park, over $100 per square foot. From our 42nd floor, the Wollman Rink looked like a postage stamp. Short-order cooks in the cafeteria whipped up eggs Benedict and toasted outsized corn muffins brushed with liquid butter. It was impossible to spend more than $1.07 for breakfast while you gazed out on Madison Avenue's uptown traffic revving up.

Years later, the cafeteria was abolished and FAO Schwarz leased the space. On Wall Street in the seventies, the prodigality of General Motors' management was an open secret. I'd rank it with F. Ross Johnson's RJR Nabisco "air force." But, after you lose share-of-market points to Honda and Toyota, you do notch in your belt. It took KKR's LBO to disperse Ross and his RJR fleet. No securities analyst ever, in print, referred to such mufti-pufti. GM became a ward of the U.S. Treasury in the 2008–'09 financial meltdown, but was a comeback with new management.

I loved frugal managers like Sam Walton, Larry Tisch, Rupert Murdoch as well as Warren Buffett, Charlie Ergen of DISH and Apple's Steve Jobs.

The Value Investor's Dilemma (Can't X-Out Growth)

Walton's achievement was that he took a prosaic business like discount retailing and turned it into a smoothly oiled powerhouse. After he eliminated the middleman distribution, he delivered for less to his heartland customers. Sears, Roebuck delivered 50 years ago but then lost it after Julius Rosenwald retired. It sold, mid-sixties, at 30 times earnings. Walton paid himself $325,000 a year, which is a hell of a lot less than most General Motors vice presidents. Tisch took $100,000. The total compensation of Walmart's 16 executive officers was less than Saul Steinberg took out of Reliance Group before it plunged into receivership.

Frugality pervaded even Walmart's annual report; no fancy photography. It was 20 pages on recycled paper. Sam's symbolism was just plain folks delivering the best for less. "You come in and see us, you hear."

Think of all the crap financial publications put us through cataloguing the filthy rich. Only a handful of Wall Streeters made it by investing their own money. The secret words are "other people's money." This holds for the great real estate and LBO fortunes that used bank debt and limited partners' capital. If you want to make a billion, the easiest route is to borrow a billion. Just convince the banks and investment bankers that you're the jockey they should bet on.

Very few of the super-rich founded their own companies. Some notable exceptions: Jeff Bezos of Amazon, Facebook's Mark Zuckerberg, Bill Gates of Microsoft and Ray Kroc of McDonald's, now gone. Include Sam Walton of Walmart, Ernest and Julio Gallo and Messrs. Hewlett and Packard, as well as Murdoch, Steve Jobs and Larry Ellison of Oracle. For them, wealth was an abstraction of entrepreneurial energy and love of their business world.

For passive investors to single out entrepreneurial geniuses who have identical agendas with their shareholders is difficult but not impossible. You start with annual reports, hopefully plain-talking documents radiating energy and results. Frugality counts, but even more is the capacity for surprising you. Share buybacks of more than 10% catch my eye. Audacious acquisitions that are non-dilutive get triggered near bottom-of-industry cycles.

Buffett's purchase of BNSF and Tisch's buy of a major fire and casualty un-

Train to Outslug the Market

derwriter were duplicated a year later by Sandy Weill of Prime America. Sandy bought a big tranche of Travelers below book value and followed with the cash purchase of American Express's brokerage business, Shearson, also a non-dilutive deal, and then finally Citicorp, a merger of equals which proved too big to get your hands around. You need to figure out when to stop and get off the bus.

I try to separate what's pejorative from what's real waste and hurtful to our economic well-being. GM and IBM each pissed away at least $25 billion in shareholder equity during the eighties. Both closed sizable plants they had just recently finished paying for. These two enterprises at their peak employed over a million, boasted impeccable balance sheets and paid out half their earnings to shareholders. It took a $25 billion write-off in 1992 for GM to issue its annual report simply in black and white on recycled paper. They even kept it under 50 pages. The demise of GM and IBM anguished hundreds of thousands of families much more than all the heartburn dished out by dot-com blowups a decade later when code-writing computer nerds dropped off the screen.

At the core of any successful investment is the leverage inherent in entrepreneurial management. Donald Trump actually reversed this schema by leveraging the public with junk bonds to bail himself out of moribund casino investments that had turned sour. Michael Thomas aptly pegged Trump as "The Prince of Swine." The passive investor needed street smarts to pick and choose his jockeys early on. Beware of grandiosity. Jokingly, Ted Turner once told me if he could raise the capital, he'd buy the Atlantic and Pacific Oceans. Later, he vied for CBS but lost out to Larry Tisch.

Smart value investing is not just buying stocks that sell at a lower price-earnings ratio than the market or at a discount to book value or just a modest premium. There has to be an energizing force to leverage earnings power. Mid-2020, viable value themes in the market abounded: autos, department stores, defense contractors, domestic oils. Even tech houses like Apple and Microsoft, long-distance telecommunications carriers like Verizon and AT&T and railroads like Canadian Pacific weren't too pricey during 2020's spring rally.

Value investing is always a moving target. Following the '82 recession, price-to-book value produced exceptional returns but proved useless after the recovery when the market sold at a 50% premium to asset value. The ratio of enterprise value to EBITDA and price-to-revenue models also showed value added.

The most telling variable for me still is price to free cash flow. When the free-cash-flow yield rests above 6%, I get interested. Apple was a prime case but there were many more in the media sector like Comcast, 21st Century Fox and Walt Disney. Boeing was a prime candidate until it blew itself up. My projection had been free cash flow exploding to near $15 a share, over a 10% yield. Halliburton got my money, spring of 2020.

Growth vs. Value Sector Comparisons

Year	S&P 500 Value	S&P 500 Growth	Spread Growth vs. Value
2001	-11.7%	-12.7%	-1.0%
2002	-20.9	-23.6	-2.7
2003	31.8	25.7	-6.1
2004	15.7	6.1	-9.6
2005	5.8	4.0	-1.8
2006	20.8	11.0	-9.8
2007	2.0	9.1	7.1
2008	-39.2	-34.9	4.3
2009	21.2	31.6	10.4
2010	15.1	15.1	0.0
2011	-0.5	4.7	5.1
2012	17.7	14.6	-3.1
2013	32.0	32.8	0.8
2014 Through June 9th	6.7	6.4	-0.3
Annualized Performance 2001–June 9, 2014	5.1%	4.8%	-0.3%

Train to Outslug the Market

In this growth vs. value table, I was amazed by how close they came out over decades-long measurement. But, year by year, variances can be extreme at inflection points in the market. Growth did much better coming out of the 2009 recession. In 2006, with the economy booming, particularly in financial stocks, value outdid growth. As an investor, I make no distinction between growth and value stocks. It's an elusive concept that doesn't deal with where we are in an economic cycle or whether the market is overvaluing or undervaluing growth stocks. Mid-2014, aside from the internet, growth properties were on the cheap side and overshadowed the value sector, big time. Its why Warren Buffett underperformed through 2019.

Weighting of Critical Value Factors

	Dividend Discount Model	Price / Book	Forward P/E	Dividend Yield	Price / Sales	Enterprise Value / EBITDA	Enterprise Value / Free Cash Flow	TOTAL
Core Old Economy 1	30%	10%	0%	15%	10%	10%	25%	100%
Growth Sectors 2	10	0	10	10	10	20	40	100%
Telecommunications	20	10	0	10	40	10	10	100%
Financials	40	25	15	20	0	0	0	100%
Utilities	0	40	0	0	20	20	20	100%
Defense	40	20	20	10	10	0	0	100%

1 Autos & housing, capital equipment, commodities, transports and energy.
2 Technology, healthcare, consumer cyclicals and consume staples.

Because most financial stocks, specifically banks and brokerage houses, are perennially leveraged to their capital base, I use hard book value as a benchmark, net of goodwill. You buy brokerage houses and banks near book value and bang 'em out at 1.5 times book. Great opportunities opened up during the financial panic of 2008–'09 and the coronavirus scare early in 2020. Banks needed a steeper yield curve to become market leaders. JPMorgan Chase, Citigroup and

The Value Investor's Dilemma (Can't X-Out Growth)

Bank of America remained somewhat preggies, capable of 5% daily bounces.

Any property that I think is misperceived with huge free cash flow coming, gets my money. The stock must have one more thing—rising earnings or at least the expectation of a turnaround in the numbers.

Be early! Wait too long to dot the i's and cross your t's and most of the upside is history. Mid-2020, I carried over 20% of my portfolio in energy master-limited partnerships that yielded anywhere from 8% to 15%. EPD covered its payout of distributable cash flow, yielding 8%. Stocks like Enterprise Products Partners were a layup. My crash helmet was buckled. I believed the history of interest rates was on my side.

High levels of capital spending and a rapidly rising share base, often because of deal mania, are telltale signs of a management going out of control. The dot-coms were good examples in the growth sector. Currently, Facebook, Salesforce.com, Twitter, even Google and Apple are overpaying in cash on notched-in deals.

Curiously, when NASDAQ fell below 2,000 in March 2001, I started applying some of the same yardsticks to growth stocks. For former growth icons like Cisco, EMC, Hewlett-Packard, Oracle and Intel we used price-to-revenues as a yardstick.

Contrapuntally, my most successful investments in the tech meltdown were in tobacco, HMOs and insurance as players fled growth stocks. HMOs were tarnished by years of federal and state regulation as well as analyst fears that medical-cost ratios couldn't be contained. But the rising-rate structure prevailed. WellPoint, out on the West Coast, sold at 15 times earnings with a 15% growth rate. Anytime you find a company at one times its growth rate and you like the management and its business, jump in whether it's perceived as a growth stock or value paper. WellPoint had converged. They could be bought by all money managers without causing style drift.

Mid-2020, practically all of technology had reverted back to the high-growth sector, particularly internet houses and cloud-computer operators. Start with Microsoft, a market capitalization over a trillion, and work your way down

Train to Outslug the Market

to Cisco Systems, Intel, Micron Technology, even IBM. The pivotal issue is—can these properties renew themselves or at least maintain sufficient reinvestment earnings, buy back stock and do deals?

Microsoft, after a double, was still investable mid-2020 along with Facebook, but Amazon, a 5% position, remained for me inscrutable. I missed the snapback in financials because I couldn't construe a major recovery coming for interest rates. The flat yield curve in Treasuries bothered me. I bought more BB high-yield bonds where yield disparity with 10-year Treasuries stood near 500 basis points. Fear of deep recession eased mid-2020. The rally in junk paper made me complacent, that there was more to come, a dangerous tendency.

Growth vs. value? I've solved for X with my barbell construct: Microsoft and Facebook on one end. Other end is Halliburton and Enterprise Products Partners, which yields 8%. Most everyone fears the MLP leveraged capital structure. When oil futures turned to dust spring of 2020, overleveraged MLPs like Energy Transfer sold to yield 16%. Hardly anyone believed its distributable cash flow could be sustainable. ET based out below $4 a share, then doubled in a couple of months. The snapback in oil futures did the trick. I felt there was more coming.

Upward Mobility Is a DIY Process

This graph on wealth mobility says it loud 'n' clear. If you were born in 1940, chances are your earnings power turned greater than your parents'. But, 50 years later, upward income mobility had declined to 50% of the workforce. My niece who recently graduated from medical school carries a $250,000 negative balance on her student loan account. The hospital she works for has told her she'll never earn more than $120,000 per annum. She can't afford to buy a new car.

I remember 1940 quite clearly. Economists use 1940 as the date the Depression was ending in the country, thanks to the step-up in armaments production and employment rolls. The Sosnoffs remained mired in poverty. We lived on baked potatoes topped with sour cream, most dinners.

I was happily mastering long division. My teacher, Miss Salt, was an Irish spinster who used her hands. Crack, crack, across the face because I was a "sneak, sneak, sneak." Her voice modulated upward with each "sneak." Grade school was intensive. Our principal, Miss Barr, pretty much discovered phonics and introduced it in our beginning-reading programs.

I remember 1943 when Oklahoma! swept Broadway. My older brother George bought the album for $2.98 and played it incessantly on our wind-up phonograph. The corn wasn't "as high as an elephant's eye" on Sherman Avenue. But, without any sense of it, we were an upwardly mobile family. My elder brother Gene distinguished himself at Yale Law School while my mother went back to school and finished with a PhD in psychology. Mother built an

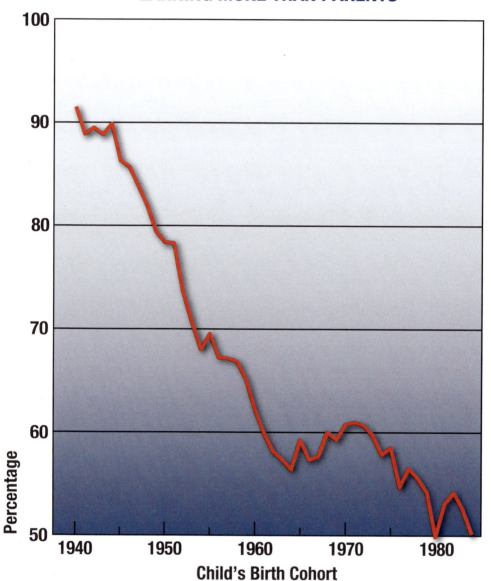

Figure 8
Source: *The Fading American Dream,* NBER Working Paper Series, Raj Chetty, et al.

Upward mobility Is a DIY Process

active practice treating children with reading disorders. Her contribution was reading disorders were psychologically based. She used play therapy to uncover neurosis.

When I hear talk of cutbacks in higher education, I think of LaGuardia, my favorite mayor of New York City. Fiorello opened special high schools at the height of the Great Depression, 1936. I attended the High School of Music and Art while my brother went to Stuyvesant in the forties.

While there was some upward mobility for the workforce in the sixties and seventies, the power of the United Auto Workers Union topped out mid-seventies. Domestic manufacturers busily relocated plants abroad in low-labor-cost countries. Hourly wage gains running as high as 7%, early seventies, topped out. Jimmy Hoffa no longer called the shots. Rather, Paul Volcker looked at the country's inflationary bias and decided to end it with drastic interest rates, as high as 15%.

The previous chart shows upward mobility by 1980 had dropped to 50%. I understand the changing dynamics but am still shocked by the drastic downward trajectory. Where is the new LaGuardia, and how secure today is free tuition at city and state colleges? I dunno.

Unexpectedly, the locus of my wealth decades ago shifted to my art collecting. I found early recognition paid off at a greater rate of compounding than even the Microsofts and Amazons. I was a little late for Warhols, Stellas and Basquiat pieces but not Baselitz and Kiefer. Later on, Cecily Brown, Ed Ruscha and Jenny Saville, whose work, initially, was hard to like—bloodied faces, obese nudes, battered bodies. A decade ago, Saville's work barely sold at auction, but it proved analogous to Impressionist work early on—revolting. What I have experienced is what's deemed too ugly mellows over time—say, 25 years.

I never bought a work of art as an investment. Rather, I assumed nobody's as stupid as I am. I'd mark down the piece as near worthless. Past decade, if I had spent as much time in the art world as in financial market pursuits, I'd be an outstanding statistic in some economist's table on wealth distribution.

Train to Outslug the Market

Sixty years ago, Bell Laboratories invented the transistor and licensed it to all comers. IBM was notable then for its great electric typewriter. The 360 computer was years away. My first job on Wall Street, the house gave me a portable adding machine to do my numbers. I taught myself to use a slide rule for multiplication and division. Partners left over from 1929 termed us as statisticians.

Yes, there was Polaroid coming out with color film. The Street's captivating concept then was razor blades, not cloud computing. Gillette's stainless blade was the standout along with Procter & Gamble's Pampers, Diet Coke and Philip Morris's filtered ciggies—all subject to daily repeatable usage. Later Syntex's "The Pill" took over along with Boeing's 707 jet aircraft.

Energy now weighs in at 3.3%, less than the market cap for Amazon or Apple. Only utilities and real estate are lesser weightings. Back in 1990, technology was a sliver of the index, maybe 5%, comparable with financials, now under a 10% weighting. Dominant components were industrials and consumer staples like Coca-Cola.

General Electric and Exxon Mobil held number one and three positions, 1991, in the S&P 500 Index. General Electric's market cap was $415 billion, but is now an insignificant number. In the 2014 standings, Microsoft stood at $402 billion. Apple was numero uno at $667 billion. Currently, they are 1.5 trillion to 2 trillion. But, despite all the good news, Apple has appreciated under 50%. Microsoft is ahead 150%. My money rests on Microsoft. Apple, for me, is too tough to model, particularly mobile phone unit volume and pricing.

Management dynamics count. Wells Fargo six years ago was a decidedly bigger market valuation then JPMorgan Chase. No longer. Morgan is twice the size of Wells Fargo, which was a major holding of Berkshire Hathaway. General Electric then was the sole industrial left in the top 10 before collapsing into single digits. Reserves for long-tailed assets were woefully inadequate. Too many acquisitions proved disasters which left goodwill to be written off.

Reminded me of American International Group, WorldCom and Enron. All creative accounting jobs that fooled the Street for years and years. When

Upward mobility Is a DIY Process

macroeconomic forces are scary or a big yawn, the market overfocuses on story stocks that can self-destruct.

While writing this piece I watched Schlumberger bounce nearly 10%, so I bought more Halliburton. Forget about the concept of owning quality paper. Junk bonds get my money, not AAA corporates yielding under 3%. Leave Coca-Cola to Warren Buffett. It's off 25%, the cola story played out in terms of per capita consumption.

The BKX Index of bank stocks was cut in half during the opening quarter of 2020. Our financial world is willful, capricious and overreactive to change. Make a mistake and you'll go shirtless. Even Facebook and Alphabet, which are balance-sheet powerhouses with position on the board, are no higher than a year ago. Halliburton, then much beloved, ticked at $30, not nine bucks. Citigroup, from its yearend high, lost 50% of its value. No reentry for me until I can build an income statement to believe in.

Normally, a one-sided reading is a warning sign of overvaluation. But, at 9:30 a.m. as the animals spring from their cages, there's Amazon, up 50 points. My mind drifted elsewhere. Was it time for great franchises like Walt Disney, victimized by the coronavirus shutdown? I took a probe. What about American Express and JPMorgan Chase? Comeback? Comeback? Soon, but not yet.

Nobody delves into the widening gap between GAAP and non-GAAP reported earnings, particularly for tech houses. Here the difference is in excessive stock grants to management and key employees.

The majority of the workforce for most retailers are part-timers with no leverage. Even middle-class families remain financially makeshift because of low net-worth accumulation. Typically, net worth is divided between home ownership and pension fund assets with the total approaching $100,000. Home equity runs around $75,000, but just $25,000 in pension fund assets, and figure the home mortgage at $25,000.

It's hard for me to compute more than $50,000 if available to invest here even if you mortgage yourself to the hilt. How many "would-be" operators can

Train to Outslug the Market

muster the courage to leverage themselves? Alas! There's no other way to fight your way into a new wealth category. Like Elon Musk, you need a moon shot with a good landing, or a Basquiat canvas for $2,500.

The Art of Measurement Is Tricky

**Dow Jones Industrials
Top 10 Market Capitalizations**
(July 2020)

Apple	10.11%
UnitedHealth Group	7.80%
Home Depot	6.69%
Microsoft	5.44%
Visa	5.10%
Johnson & Johnson	3.85%
Boeing	3.06%
Walmart	3.38%
Procter & Gamble	3.22%
JPMorgan Chase	2.50%
Total	**51.15%**

Notable here is the Dow Jones Industrials title is no longer descriptive of this list. A year ago, it was heavy in industrials, Boeing, a 9% position, now 3.6%. Share price shrinkage impacted Caterpillar, Dow Chemical, Exxon Mobil and others resting further down the listing. The top 10 now are mainly growth stocks like Apple, Microsoft, UnitedHealth Group, Home Depot and Johnson & Johnson. Financials like Visa, Goldman Sachs and American Express

Train to Outslug the Market

approximate a 10% weighting and do add volatility, quarterly. In short, market shifts downward for industrials cured index obsolescence and made it resemble NASDAQ.

Sixty years ago, Dow Jones was a revered name. At Merrill Lynch offices, willowy girls with trim ankles chalked up on blackboards changing prices for the Dow Thirty that they scanned on the chattering market ticker.

Mid-2020, with the Dow ticking at 26,000, a 200-point move is less than 1%, basically a random reading. The Dow dropped under 10,000 in 2001 after the tech bubble burst. At the nadir of the financial meltdown in 2009, the index based at 6,649, but by yearend 2014, breached 18,000. When interest rates approached zero, the perception was they can rest there for years to come, what we had mid-2020 was a minimal equity risk premium, a plus factor for valuation.

I construe the three market indices—Dow, NASDAQ and S&P 500—as three circus horses moving in the ring at different speeds. NASDAQ's nag is galloping, with DJIA cantering along with the S&P 500. Individual investors should rate themselves against the index that closely resembles weightings of their stocks.

Institutional investors normally use the S&P 500 for their rating benchmark. This still makes sense. But hedge fund operators who carry more volatile and smaller capitalization situations also use the S&P 500 for measurement purposes because they think it's easier to beat and results in higher performance-fee content, year-over-year. They should use the NASDAQ-100 for figuring out their performance fees. Clients are too passive on this issue. They don't get how they're being taken.

Shifts in weighting were sizable. Financials comprised 20% of the index. Industrials were still important at 15%, while growth stocks weighed in around 13%. The top 10 comprised over half the Dow's capitalization. It was a much easier index to beat if you overweighted growth stocks and deemphasized industrials and energy.

Stepping back, there is this basic fault in the index which ties weighting to market price rather than market capitalization.

The Art of Measurement Is Tricky

Dow Jones Industrials
Top 10 Market Capitalizations
(December 2014)

Visa	9.4%
Goldman Sachs	6.9%
IBM	5.8%
3M Company	5.8%
Boeing	4.7%
United Technologies	3.98%
Chevron	3.96%
Johnson & Johnson	3.88%
Travelers	3.76%
UnitedHealth Group	3.59%

By omitting Apple, Alphabet, Amazon and Microsoft, all near trillion-dollar market capitalizations, the Dow had confined itself to voluntary disrepute and near obsolescence. The NASDAQ is a better mirror of what's going on in the financial world, but is still largely ignored because it's too tough to beat in a bull market and self-destructs in a bear market. During the tech bubble of 2000–'01, NASDAQ dropped 60% over 12 months. Yearend 2001, Microsoft was the largest capitalization in the NASDAQ-100 at $344 billion. No Amazon, Alphabet and Facebook, as yet.

Own NASDAQ-100, and you're overweighted in technology and e-commerce. Top five positions account for 45% of the index's weighting. PepsiCo barely makes the list, a 2% position. Technology comprises over 25% of the S&P 500's weighting. But the NASDAQ-100 is double-weighted in technology, while Amazon carries little bottom-line earnings. Microsoft brings down plenty and sells at 1.5 times the multiple of the S&P 500 Index, a fair assessment.

NASDAQ-100
10 Largest Positions
(July 2020)

Apple	11.89%
Microsoft	11.63%
Amazon	11.02%
Facebook	4.26%
Alphabet (Class A)	3.78%
Alphabet (Class C)	3.68%
Tesla	2.42%
Intel	2.32%
Nvidia	2.28%
Netflix	2.04%

Spring of 2020, I concluded the NASDAQ top 10 were no more risky than the market, which sold at 18 times normalized earnings, nowhere in sight. I held a 14% position in Microsoft, hardly more than its index weighting. This surprised me, but gave me comfort. Not a totally outlandish bet.

Another way to construe NASDAQ-100 is you're operating as aggressively weighted as a maximum-intensity hedge fund operator. When I checked latest quarterly 13F filings, there were few operators consistently overweighted in technology. Tiger Global Management, an $18 billion fund, stood out with 30% weighted in Facebook, Microsoft, Amazon and Alibaba. Some 65% of Appaloosa's assets rested in tech houses. Duquesne's Family Office, practically all tech with special plays plus a 5% position in General Electric, which mid-2020 traded in new-low ground. Lone Pine Capital, likewise tech positioned, its top holding was 7% in Alibaba, one of my holdings.

The table on largest market capitalizations in 2001, with the exception of Microsoft, was comprised mainly of traditional names like Exxon Mobil,

The Art of Measurement Is Tricky

General Electric, even AIG and IBM. Citigroup was more than twice the market size of JPMorgan.

Contrast such old staples as Coca-Cola with a week when oil futures plunged into negative numbers while two-year Treasuries sold to yield 19 basis points and 10-year paper at 0.62%, down from over 2% in 2019. The market needed to deal with the deflationary wet blanket covering energy, industrials, financials, almost everything except technology. Amazon, Microsoft and Netflix soldiered on. Technology weighting in the S&P 500 Index mid-2020 exceeded 25%, likely to work higher.

Energy at its low weighed in at 3.3%, less than the market cap for Amazon or Apple. Only utilities and real estate showed lesser weightings. Back in 1990, technology was a sliver of the index, maybe 5%, comparable with financials, now under a 10% weighting. Dominant components were industrials and consumer staples like Coca-Cola.

A decade later, around 2000, technology and financials mushroomed into dominant sectors (See Fig. 9, p. 92). But, at the bottom of the market in 1991, tech was at a 6% weighting. Pre-bubble, 2000, iconic tech houses sold at 60 times earnings, but by 2001 had melted down to 20 times earnings. Then, players craved to own properties like Sun Microsystems and Oracle.

I was caught up in oil service plays, then as now, that energy futures would trade over $100 a barrel. Now, I'll settle for $40. Halliburton was a favored position. At least today, tech is powered by rising earnings, not just elevated price-earnings ratios, but Halliburton was capable of sprinting 15% one day in May 2020. Oil futures rose 15% on word the Saudi cutbacks in production were real and sizable.

If referencing the market against the Dow Jones Industrials, you're sort of obsolete, living in the dark ages of the 1950s, when technology as a market sector was insignificant. Let's leave the Dow Jones to broadcasters with blow-dried hair. The market is dominated by tech house paper. Apple, Microsoft, Facebook, Amazon and Alibaba. These are trillion-dollar capitalizations, more or less. They are the market.

Top 25 Stocks in the S&P 500 Index
(as of March 31, 2001)

Rank in S&P 500	Company Name	Percent of S&P	Market Value (Billions)
1	General Electric	4.1	415.8
2	Microsoft	2.8	291.0
3	ExxonMobil	2.7	280.7
4	Pfizer	2.5	258.6
5	Citigroup	2.2	225.9
6	Wal-Mart	2.2	225.6
7	AIG	1.8	186.4
8	Intel	1.7	176.8
9	Merck	1.7	175.1
10	IBM	1.6	167.6
11	SBC	1.5	151.1
12	Verizon	1.3	133.2
13	Johnson & Johnson	1.2	121.6
14	Royal Dutch Petroleum	1.2	118.9
15	Bristol Myers Squibb	1.1	116.3
16	Cisco	1.1	114.5
17	Coca-Cola	1.1	112.2
18	Philip Morris	1.0	105.0
19	Home Depot	1.0	100.1
20	AOL Time Warner	0.9	93.7
21	Bank of America	0.9	88.3
22	JPMorgan Chase	0.8	86.6
23	Eli Lilly	0.8	86.3
24	Wells Fargo	0.8	84.8
25	Oracle	0.8	83.8

Total   38.8

The Art of Measurement Is Tricky

(Footnote to table on previous page)

Fast-forwarding to 2014, the top 25 names in the S&P 500 Index showed markedly disparate performance, suggesting a stockpicker's game. Nobody believed the index carried wind at its back. Apple recovered, but Google trailed, Microsoft rose 20 percent. Berkshire Hathaway, a play on Buffett's 50 percent weighting in financials, rose 20 percent. Wells Fargo, up 20 percent, was a grossly overweighted position there. JPMorgan and Citigroup underperformed. Amazon dropped a snappy 20 percent and Schlumberger gave back its gain. The top 25 names in the S&P 500 mainly sell at modest price-earnings ratios, with the exception of Facebook. When market pundits wring their hands over valuation of the S&P 500, they ignore this qualification. In 2001 General Electric headed the list at 4.1%. Microsoft was a distant second. (See Figure 9, p. 92)

U.S. Steel's market value is a not-so-hefty $7 billion by comparison, a pimple on the market. In the old days there was Polaroid coming out with color film, but the Street's captivating concept was razor blades, not cloud computing. The advent of technology in the early sixties did away with the repeatable-usage concept.

Mid 2020, I owned Amazon but had more money in Halliburton, Freeport-McMoRan, and Williams. You could put them in your back pocket in terms of market capitalization. What I yearn to own are the great franchise operators like Walt Disney and American Express, both down around 40% from their highs. Nobody dodges market volatility. Throw in JPMorgan Chase but not Wells Fargo.

Train to Outslug the Market

S&P 500 SECTOR WEIGHTINGS

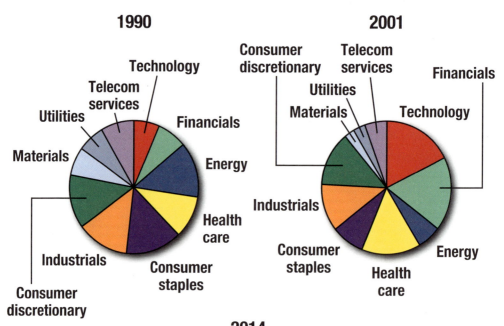

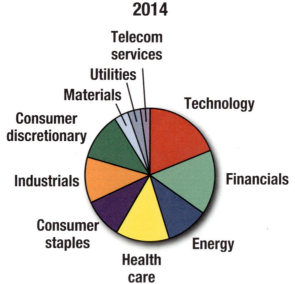

Figure 9
Source: Standard & Poors

Polite Exxon Mobil Can Bury You

Nobody ever waxed rich owning an electric utility. You wanna own them only when their cash yield is competitive with Treasuries, secure, likely to ratchet up 3% or 4% per annum. Then, fall back to sleep. Consolation is good relative performance in a bear market, but nowhere can you bank relatives.

Another kind of custodial operator walks and talks like Apple or Facebook. He tries to look proactive, but his executive floor remains dead quiet. The suits talk about "your" company in their annual report, but it's really "their" company. They do ratchet up cash dividends, but share buybacks, which I consider pro-management, turn excessive. Corporate proxy statements run 60 to 100 pages. Designed to be boring, barely readable, they must divulge all management incentives in cash, stock, insurance—whatever.

Exxon Mobil, a major market capitalization over the decades, is a great example of how to look cosmetically proper, even adventuresome, in capital spending which runs very hard to replace known oil reserves that do deplete themselves over time.

Exxon is not distinctly overleveraged like Occidental Petroleum, which after its fall yielded 6.7%, a payout ratio that was unsustainable and finally eliminated. Nobody can call Exxon Mobil a ragamuffin, but its five-year price chart was abysmal, from near par down into the forties, May 2020.

Over this term, management walked through all the motions of proactivity. But net income, 2019, ran 35% below 2018. Over 2020, they didn't come close to covering their first-half payment of $1.69 a share, up from $1.59 a year ago. Downstream results and chemicals collapsed here and abroad. Crude oil production earnings actually held up but carry only 60% of total profitability. Exxon today is a viciously cyclical piece of paper.

Capital spending runs at $30 billion, which works out to full utilization of cash flows. Average earnings for Exxon over five years through 2020 work out to around $4 a share. The stock has sold at 18 times average earnings comparable with the market's P/E ratio on forward 12 months' earnings. There is, after all, a certain symmetry to corporate valuation, historically speaking, but it's wrongly positive.

The issue is why own any custodial paper except for a cyclical bounce not anticipated by the market? This actually happened in mid-2020. The yield then on Exxon exceeded 7%, more than competitive with the market, long-term Treasuries and even high-yield debentures, but so what? In a slow growth setting, petrochemicals and gasoline price leverage is a negative, normally 40% of Exxon's operating earnings. For the first time in a decade, management didn't bump up the cash dividend. They felt the cyclicality in their bones.

There're bigger issues. Why pay up for any industrial-based property in a world where economic growth is hard to model? Look elsewhere for earnings leverage and secular growth. I consider Exxon Mobil the class act among big-capitalization industrials and energy plays. It goes through all the motions of a serious, long-term player in its field with a balance sheet that is comfortable and even now easily bears strains of cyclical variance.

In 2001, Exxon Mobil was number three in the S&P 500 Index with a market capitalization of $281 billion. By 2014, still number three, its market cap pushed $400 billion, right behind Microsoft. Mid-2020, Microsoft is a $1 trillion property, numero uno. Exxon's market cap is down to $160 billion from $324 billion, mid-2019. This is a mini-disaster for a major property.

Sooo...since 2001, Exxon Mobil management has run very hard and methodically, stayed within its operating cash flow construct—but got nowhere. Yes, they've size, but what else? Early sixties, Tom Watson in an aside told me IBM had bet the company on development of its 360 computer. (They won.)

Polite Exxon Mobil Can Bury You

EXXON MOBIL PRICE CHART

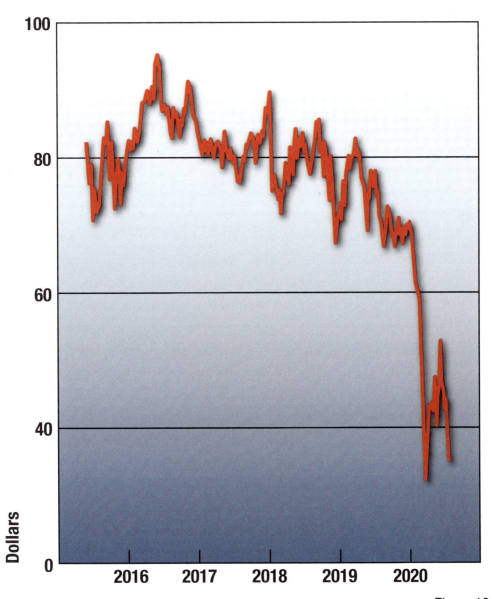

Figure 10

Train to Outslug the Market

To refresh myself, I turned to Facebook's quarterly earnings report. Facebook doesn't date back to John D. Rockefeller or IBM. Birthed in a dorm room a generation ago. Zuck still wears his same T-shirt, hopefully washed, daily.

Consider: Facebook's market capitalization, mid-2020, over $600 billion. The R&D run rate is 20% of revenues, a gutsy, unheard-of ratio even among tech houses. Operating cash flow should exceed $35 billion. Call it a 15 times multiplier. On operating cash flow, my defining metric for an internet house, Facebook at $230 was much cheaper than Exxon, maybe the entire S&P 500 Index.

The case is clear cut. Large-cap industrials and oilfield operators' records run spotty. **Investment entry points are critical.** Peak of cycle, they're poisonous and do drop a snappy 40%. Let the other guy own polite paper. Facebook and its maximum leader, Zuck, draw the worst press I've ever seen for a top 10 property. But their R&D spend rests far above Apple's. Mid-2020, Exxon was barely breaking even. Some $3 billion in quarterly cash flow had disappeared.

Journalists don't define market valuation or a company's fundamentals. Neither do most of us who hold CFAs and manage tons of capital. From its low, AT&T advanced almost 50% latest 12 months. So goes Facebook. Strange bedfellows with the common denominator of a Stupidsville consensus and a bad press.

Exxon Mobil had proudly declaimed in a recent quarterly that it raised cash dividends 6%, making it 37 years of consistent largesse. But at current earnings power, its payout is 100%. No raise coming in 2020. Not even utilities dare risk payouts more than two-thirds of earnings. I focus on the operating cash flow metric for its wherewithal to grow earnings and stock prices.

Five-year charts for prime industrials like Honeywell, 3M, United Technologies, DuPont, Dow Chemical and Deere suggest I shouldn't just beat up on Exxon Mobil. Nobody had on glad rags excepting Honeywell and Deere, who benefited from international revenue growth. Materials stocks like U.S. Steel and Alcoa sustained near-total wipeouts. You had to define railroads as internal efficiency stories, like Union Pacific and CSX, before latching onto them. By 2020, they became expensive stocks, selling at 20 times earnings.

Not that you can't make serious money in polite paper. AT&T appreciated

50% over a 12-month period, but by mid-2020 had given most of it back. **Your entry point decides whether you come out OK in a specific cyclical property.** In the spring 2020 rally, Exxon bounced from $30 to over $50, but far below its recent-years' high over $80.

Boeing's Insidious Art of Discombobulation, Elon Musk's Greed

If ever you pick up a corporate annual report to peruse and it begins with "Your company, blah, blah, blah," fling it into the wastebasket. It's not your company, no matter how many shares you own. It's their company, management's empire, to despoil. They may raise dividend payouts and buy back tranches of stock, but remember, buybacks help enhance their options value more than cash dividends, except they don't phrase it as such. It becomes "The total return to shareholders rose year-over-year, blah, blah, blah." Exxon Mobil is a good example of this mufti-pufti.

Annual reports, often composed by public relations specialists, intersperse financial patter with pretty photographs that have no resonance. You are much better off reading a public company's annual 10-K report to the SEC. It's purely factual, basically a comparison of numbers, year-over-year, no pictures. Same goes for quarterly 10-Q filings. Berkshire Hathaway's 10-K goes on and on for 49 pages of comparative numbers and small-type footnotes. It's a slog but worth doing if you care to break down Berkshire into operating components and comparisons.

Way back, jet aircraft enabled me to step into six-digit gains. When I telephoned Pop to give him the good news—I was a millionaire, age 29—he wouldn't believe me. "Bah! It's not possible, Martin, you're exaggerating." Guts brought glory. I toured Boeing's Renton, Washington, plant on their loaner bicycle, talking to aircraft assemblers. I sensed the situation was open-ended.

Wall Street, early sixties, exploded into its age of discovery. While Warren

Buffett found American Express, good for 58 years, I got to know players in semiconductors like Fairchild Camera and Motorola. Buffett stayed allergic to tech houses—even today, no internet and e-commerce plays like Amazon and Facebook.

Fast-forward to Boeing's 2019 proxy statement to see how management had rewarded itself for the stock's outstanding performance that year. Largesse was ample. Fifty years ago, when you measured management salaries and add-ons against the average worker's pay, the ratio was rarely above 10 to 1. These days it can run as high as 50 to 1 before adding in executive compensation for bonuses and stock grants.

Proxy statements do run up to 100 pages long. Corporate management hires specialist consultant firms with unctuous names that then bless management's self-rewarded largesse as appropriate, certainly not excessive by any means, particularly stock grants and long-term options.

The Boeing proxy report ran to 81 pages filled with corporatese. I finally got to page 51 for the numbers on management compensation. I have no fault with the present composition of Boeing's board of directors, which includes Caroline Kennedy and accomplished executives in the aerospace and financial services sectors. It's critical that the new chairman of the board is an independent. Average compensation for board members ranges over $300,000, with accumulated stock-compensation benefits ranging over 50,000 units for some long-term directors.

Holders of 5% or more of Boeing's stock include T. Rowe Price, BlackRock and the Vanguard Group, all long-term players. At the first whiff of fish, I banged out my Boeing position, and I'll probably never come back.

I see a new clause on drawbacks in compensation based on the safety of its products and services. The former CEO, Dennis Muilenburg, who was cashiered at yearend 2019, retrospectively could be viewed as slurring over basic safety issues to push forward on certification of the 737 MAX aircraft model.

I read through this horror of a proxy statement that was obviously designed to be boring, unreadable and in such small type, which seemed to contract as the issues under discussion got more and more complicated and obtuse. I may be the only idiot in the western world who put himself under torture to read through this proxy report by Boeing, all 81 pages.

The number of ways management, teamed with its consultant, devised to enhance future net worth made my eyes cross. Preliminaries are cosmetic as to salaries and compensation of its board of directors. First off, I like Larry Kellner, Boeing's new board chairman, who for over a decade ran Continental Airlines. I've now reviewed 17 proxy pages.

A company deceptively titled Pay Governance is Boeing's compensation consultant. Principal components of management compensation put base salary at 14% of a manager's total compensation. Then add annual incentives targeted at 17% of compensation, performance-based. Then, some 69% of total compensation. This is mainly tied to present performance goals centering on free cash flow, revenue growth, core earnings per share and total shareholder returns.

Short of holding a certificate as a chartered financial analyst, there's no way a shareholder can devise that such a compensation package makes any sense. As a money manager, I'd look at this future pay package with a gimlet eye. Boeing, as a stock, was pushing toward $500 a share before the first 737 MAX crash—no survivors. Let management first prove that it can ride out all the capital calls coming from grounded aircraft, order cancellation and an airline industry that could take years for full recovery from the country's locked-down condition and space requirements between passengers.

Total management compensation already in place counts up to $18 million for a few executives. After reviewing what's called nonqualified deferred compensation and an executive supplemental-savings plan, I threw in the towel and put down my magnifying glass to uncross my eyes.

I didn't read about their executive-layoff plan, but I did glance at the pay-ratio wordage which was imposed on the corporate world by the Dodd-Frank Wall Street Reform and Consumer Protection Act. Total compensation for Boeing's median employee counted up to $158,800, while the annual compensation of its headman, now departed, was $14,250,195, some 90 times that of

Boeing's Insidious Art of Discombobulation, Elon Musk's Greed

COMPENSATION OF EXECUTIVE OFFICERS

Summary Compensation Table

The following table sets forth information regarding compensation for each of our 2019 named executive officers.

Name and Principal Position	Year	Salary ($)[1]	Stock Awards ($)[2]	Non-Equity Incentive Plan Compensation ($)[3]	Change in Pension Value and Nonqualified Deferred Compensation Earnings ($)[4]	All Other Compensation ($)[5]	Total ($)
Dennis A. Muilenburg	2019	2,013,846	7,246,100[6]	—	2,790,155	2,200,094	14,250,195
Former President and	2018	1,700,000	7,330,916	13,076,350	—	1,284,921	23,392,187
Chief Executive Officer	2017	1,690,769	5,775,049	8,450,270	1,549,137	985,191	18,450,416
Gregory D. Smith	2019	1,128,846	2,430,699	—	411,242	545,016	4,515,803
Chief Financial Officer and	2018	1,032,462	2,550,173	4,574,957	—	524,466	8,682,058
Executive Vice President,	2017	974,308	11,779,769	3,782,592	241,461	447,484	17,225,614
Enterprise Performance and Strategy;							
Former Interim President and							
Chief Executive Officer							
Stanley A. Deal	2019	934,423	1,732,642	—	830,045	708,196	4,205,306
Executive Vice President,	2018	793,904	1,299,478	2,072,832	—	339,332	4,505,546
President and Chief Executive Officer,	2017	658,154	5,605,346	1,783,236	457,084	1,310,358	9,814,178
Commercial Airplanes							
Timothy J. Keating	2019	695,192	3,016,610	—	322,739	335,843	4,370,384
Executive Vice President,							
Government Operations							
J. Michael Luttig	2019	984,385	1,930,360[7]	—	3,841,126	549,048	7,304,919
Former Executive Vice President,	2018	959,346	1,907,572	4,325,735	—	617,945	7,810,598
Counselor and Advisor to the Board of	2017	930,385	1,819,983	3,806,282	356,410	473,447	7,386,507
Directors							
Kevin G. McAllister	2019	1,230,007	2,045,063[8]	—	—	15,154,248	18,429,318
Former Executive Vice President,	2018	1,043,404	2,131,531	3,934,889	—	566,333	7,676,157
President and Chief Executive Officer,	2017	1,012,231	3,499,936	2,187,011	—	520,120	7,219,298
Commercial Airplanes							

(1) Amounts reflect base salary paid in the year, before any deferrals at the executive's election and including salary increases effective during the year, if any. For Messrs. Muilenburg and McAllister, the amounts shown include $313,846 and $131,546, respectively, in payment of accrued but unused vacation in connection with them ceasing to be employed by the Company in 2019.

(2) Amounts reflect the aggregate grant date fair value of PBRSUs and RSUs granted in the year computed in accordance with FASB ASC Topic 718. These amounts are not paid to or realized by the executive. If the maximum level of performance were to be achieved for the PBRSUs granted in 2019, the grant date value for those PBRSUs would be $7,245,862 for Mr. Muilenburg, $2,430,822 for Mr. Smith, $1,732,706 for Mr. Deal, $1,303,958 for Mr. Keating, $1,930,304 for Mr. Luttig, and $2,044,948 for Mr. McAllister. The grant date fair value of each PBRSU and RSU award in 2019 is set forth in the 2019 Grants of Plan-Based Awards table on page 53. Messrs. Muilenburg, Luttig, and McAllister forfeited some or all of these awards when they ceased being employed by the Company. For additional information, see footnotes 6-8 to this table.

Figure 11
Source: Corporate Proxy, Boeing 2019

the average employee. This is about as rich as it gets. I gave up after page 62, excepting notice that Lawrence Kellner, Boeing's new chairman, owns beneficially just 2,500 shares, a little more than Caroline Kennedy's 1,571 shares. Not exactly a make-or-break condition for them.

The SEC needs bracing on lack of sensitivity and control over corporate proxy statements as presented to shareholders. Management's compensation of all kinds should be pushed to the front of their document, not buried on page 60. Regulators need to prescribe size of type, at least nine point. I shouldn't need a magnifying glass to clarify their take.

On page 38 of its proxy report, you find years of overly indulgent headman compensation spelled out. Dennis Muilenburg's package in 2019 totted up to $23.4 million on a salary base of $1.7 million. Over three years, his take was some $57 million. Serious money. Following on, CFO Gregory Smith took home $32 million. Did the apparent press to certify the 737 MAX have any connection with prospective largesse? Maybe. Outside directors do step into such snafu situations, but they're always late. You can't remain collegial, as long as possible. There should be a three-year giveback on such incentives.

Boeing as a stock gave back past 24 months' upside. Pre-crashes, it ticked at $450. As a shareholder then, I hypothesized a $500 price tag 12 months out, but after the news Boeing dropped to $300, then to $200. Its market capitalization was pared by $200 billion. When your company's stock drops from $450 to $350, there's no case for more than salary, and tenure should become an issue on the boardroom table.

Then I turned to Tesla's proxy report. I was somewhat refreshed to see top executives' salaries ranged no higher than $300,000 and their ages ranged from 35 to 48, for the elder, Elon Musk. There are no annual bonus provisions or severance payouts. No compensation consultants were retained publicly during 2019.

Actually, April 2020, base salaries were reduced by 30%, something I haven't run across anywhere else in the corporate world in response to marked reversals in the pandemic world. Elon Musk was granted stock options on over five million shares, 5% of Tesla's outstanding base in 10 equal vesting periods.

An additional performance award set in 2018 provided for options on over 20 million shares if specific performance goals were met over an eight-year period. Exercise price set at $350 a share. Musk's ownership, end of 2019, was 38.6 million or 20.8% of shares outstanding. Mid-2020, Musk chose to practically double his equity interest going forward—at the expense of shareholder dilution. *¿Quién sabe?* Enough is enough, Elon.

I award the palm to Salesforce.com's proxy, some 135 pages long, filled with a variety of incentive plans for management and employees. Because the variance between GAAP and non-GAAP earnings has gone past my cutoff point of 20% per annum, I won't invest in Salesforce, and missed out on a good-acting stock past year. Discipline is discipline. I won't change my spots until they change theirs.

What all this comes down to is just so long as you fully disclose everything you decide to do, you can do it. Where is the SEC on all this? Nowhere. No standards or guidelines on what's appropriate and what's rapacious. Wall Street's houses go along because they earn huge fees on corporate finance underwriting and deal activity. No house analyst dares raise the issue of a yawning variance between GAAP and non-GAAP earnings numbers.

It took two disasters for Boeing's 737 MAX to get its headman terminated, but no clawback on past years' incentive compensation. The art of proxy statement lawyerly development has gone too far, but nobody speaks up because nobody cares to read up or speak up.

14

Internet and e-Commerce Paper: Shadow Boxing in the Dark

Tech's Five-Year Price Run

	Mid-2015	Mid-2020	Percentage Gain
Amazon	500	2,436	386%
Facebook	80	235	195%
Alphabet	600	1,400	130%
Microsoft	40	183	360%
Alibaba	75	200	170%
S&P 500 Index	2,000	3,000	50%
NASDAQ-100 Index	5,000	10,000	100%

What surprised me was Microsoft outperformed all properties excepting Amazon. My five growthies, Amazon, Facebook, Alphabet, Microsoft and Alibaba, handily beat the market's 50% gain. If not overweighted in tech you probably lagged the market over five years. This certainly was Warren Buffett's experience. He did own some IBM, a non-performer that he batted out of his list. Apple is his surrogate for tech, but a fairly recent addition. Looking ahead, the pivotal issue for such big-capitalization properties is whether earnings momentum at mid-teens or better is in the cards.

Building income statements for these five operators is near impossible. How to gauge advertising demand at Facebook, e-commerce revenues for Amazon and Alibaba? Analyst projections are horseback numbers. Jeff Bezos plays

Internet and e-Commerce Paper: Shadow Boxing in the Dark

with his analyst fraternity. His numbers, always low-ball, are laughable and useless. All said, Amazon brings very little to its bottom line. Analysts look out at least three years to rationalize Amazon's stock price. They invoke metrics like operating cash flow, price to EBITDA, free cash flow yield—anything but earnings per share.

Bezos, perennially, finds new ways to spend big blocks of capital. What saves him is Amazon's balance sheet is underleveraged and operating cash flow is a big number. These are the only metrics I check out, quarterly. They keep me placed in the stock.

I'm a numbers man, massaging corporate income statements and balance sheets over some 60 years. Numbers, not headmen's rhetoric, tell the story. They sing as in Amazon, Apple and Alibaba or don't sing as in Macy's, General Electric, even Exxon Mobil, a polite disaster facing a dividend schmeiss next year.

I can look at a corporate balance sheet for 60 seconds and tell you whether it's undercapitalized, overcapitalized or even precariously perched for a bankruptcy filing within 12 months if numbers don't wax better.

One of the great circle jerks on the Street is the quarterly management-guidance séance for analysts. Managements today are smart enough only to handhold their constituency up to the point of projecting next quarter's numbers within a narrow range.

Jeff Bezos at Amazon does this with gusto. Bezos never projects Amazon earning more money in the coming quarter than in the past quarter or that revenues grow much at all. Such nonsense ensures analyst projections for revenues and earnings never match reality. The company then attains an upside numbers surprise, worth its weight in gold.

Nobody ever gets his numbers right on a trillion to $2 trillion market capitalization. Start with Apple and work down to Microsoft, Amazon, Alphabet, even Facebook and then Alibaba. The great irony in the bull market for technology paper is that nobody can sharp-pencil earnings numbers or even build a credible income model that goes out three to five years.

105

Train to Outslug the Market

As such stocks levitate, say 300% over five years, everyone gradually discards his earnings-per-share model and deals rather with multiples of revenues, multipliers of EBITDA or in my case operating cash flow. **My focus on operating cash flow is that at least this is the wherewithal available to management for building out their core competences.**

I use the multiple of free-cash-flow yield too, for the same reason. Free-cash-flow yields ranging from 5% to 10% comfort me in my picks. In Facebook's case, I'm amazed by their research spend, which approximates 20% of revenues. But, they tell you nothing about research priorities, so it's a raw stat.

Balance sheets are useless except for projecting how much stock the company in question could buy back. This was an important consideration in analyzing Apple, with its colossal redundant capital, but not so usable for Amazon, Facebook and Alibaba. In Alibaba's case, they are losing, perennially, billions covering initiatives in cloud computing and the entertainment sector, with no hint on future profitability.

They tell us nothing about their 33% holding in Ant Group, which is a Far Eastern octopus in the making—covering money management, credit cards and automated payments by consumers. Next five years, I see Ant built out and capitalized by the market at over $500 billion, maybe equivalent to Alibaba's present market cap of $600 billion.

When reading Alibaba's quarterly reports, first thing that strikes me is the sheer magnitude of its consumer franchise. I remember being wowed by Polaroid's and Xerox's franchises expressed in volumetric revenue growth, operating profit enhancement and bottom-line earnings. This was 60 years ago and competing technologies practically destroyed the sixties growthies over a span of under five years, not decades. Diversification initiatives proved stillborn.

Catch this bunch of Alibaba numbers: Quarterly revenues up 34%. There are 874 million mobile active users, up 28 million year-over-year. Operating income plus 42% and EBIDTA up 30%. Non-GAAP net up 28% to $5.6 billion and non-GAAP free cash flow at $5.2 billion. Operating cash flow at a

$7 billion quarterly run rate. Earnings per share plus 18%. They are still losing billions in cloud computing and entertainment initiatives. Using my shorthand, I'd put annualized operating cash flow conservatively at $30 billion. Alibaba justifies its $600 billion market value.

Dissecting Amazon's operating cash flow we see the latest 12 months' numbers rose 42% to $51.2 billion. On my horseback numbers, Amazon sells at 25 times forward 12 months' operating cash flow, pricier than Alibaba, but it controls a hugely profitable cloud-computing division and carries a foreign revenue base approximating $100 billion that as yet earns zilch. For how long do you sacrifice gross margins, building your footprint? Jeff Bezos tells us nothing. You need a 25 multiplier on forward-operating cash flow to rationalize Amazon's current price. I'm OK with such valuation metrics but I own more Alibaba than Amazon. Net, net, it's a cheaper piece of paper. So far, easier to follow, quarter over quarter.

Maybe I should move to Hong Kong, buy a bunch of Ant Group, then watch 'em build out their franchise next five years.

There's one last way of comparing Alibaba to Amazon. Forget about per-share numbers, but look at the sheer magnitude of their business footprints in e-commerce and cloud computing.

Conveniently, the opening sentence of all Amazon financial reports covers operating cash flow numbers for trailing 12 months. At yearend 2019, this was $38.5 billion, up 25%. My reasoning for singling out this metric is that it adumbrates the business's health as well as providing the wherewithal for reinvestment and future growth. If you project near $50 billion for operating cash flow in 2020 you can rationalize a price of at least $2,000 for Amazon. It's enough to keep you in the stock but not enough to make you buy more. And yet, at midyear the stock ticked at $2,600. Who knew?

Looking at my earlier 2020 projection of earnings per share in the low thirties (which won't be met), Amazon was selling at 70 times earnings, an unusable number for anyone involved in the stock. Nobody ever said growth stock investing was simplistic. You had to believe that e-commerce profit margins

Train to Outslug the Market

finally would approach Walmart or Costco numbers, but it wouldn't happen overnight. Maybe in five years.

In short (no pun), Amazon remains unanalyzable, despite a market capitalization, August 2020, at $1.7 trillion. Microsoft's market capitalization equals Amazon's and is easily mappable in terms of earnings and cash flow. Microsoft sold no more than 30 times earnings, a fair premium over the S&P 500 Index. Because it's understandable, I've twice as much invested in Microsoft as in Amazon.

Surprised by what I found. In cloud computing, Amazon has built out a major presence. Amazon Web Services is now importantly profitable. June quarter's run rate for revenues was $10.8 billion with operating income rising over 50% to $3.3 billion, a serious number. For Alibaba, a late cloud arrival, we still see red ink. Revenues here latest quarter at $1.7 billion, but still losing money. It's big in China, but nowhere else a worldwide contender.

In e-commerce, the story flip-flops. Amazon's revenue run rate in North America has surged to the $200 billion level with operating income now running at $8 billion. The international sector, approaching a $100 billion revenue base, turned profitable in the June quarter. Maybe, we're looking at a forward run rate over $1 billion, annually.

Alibaba's e-commerce footprint remains awesome in magnitude and profitability. Annual-active consumers in China reached 874 million at midyear, the base still growing. Revenues, up 34% June quarter, look like an annual run rate approaching $100 billion with operating income north of $20 billion, maybe $25 billion for non-GAAP net income.

So Alibaba boasts a sizable, consistent earnings footprint in e-commerce, weighing in at $25 billion. Amazon, benefiting from shut-in consumers, maybe at an $8 billion level. Boiled down, I'd construe Alibaba remains the premier world e-commerce operator. Amazon today is more of a cloud-computer contender with an e-commerce sector that needed Covid-19 to turn much more than marginally profitable.

Down the road, Alibaba's Ant Group investment could become the tail wagging the dog on asset-enhancement valuation. Alibaba is easier to model and probably a better investment but not by a wide margin. Own 'em both in a two-for-one ratio favoring Alibaba unless you think the Chinese economy turns into a burned-out case.

As a stock, past five years, Amazon left Alibaba in the dust. This could reverse next couple of years.

Lemme go on to Facebook, where Zuckerberg and company have endured a hostile financial press for a couple of years. But, no impact on valuation. Actually, Facebook, past 12 months was almost a double. The financial press for me is a contrary indicator. They never put emphasis on the right syllable.

The first Facebook metric I look at is advertising revenues. If going along at a good clip, chances are the stock is levitating, too. Advertising so far is undiminished, despite some advertisers' boycotts. Facebook coasts along at a 25% revenue growth clip. This is breathtaking during the COVID-19 meltdown, which so impacted traditional retailing.

A singular line in the expense column is research and development running at an annualized rate over $16 billion or 20% of revenues. R&D at 20% of revenues is nearly unheard of, even historically, in the high-tech world. Nobody picks up on this outsized metric. Zuck gives out no details on spending specifics, so let's hope he connects. Eye-catching, too, is the scale-up in employment at year-over-year growth of 28%. These may be largely spear carriers but still an enormous addition.

Unlike Amazon, Facebook gives out plenty of stock to productive employees. Share-based compensation runs at a $5 billion clip, over 20% of pretax income. This is my cut-off point for investment consideration. Let's call Facebook's operating cash flow annualized above $25 billion. On its current 2020 market capitalization of $710 billion, call it over 25 times 2020's operating cash flow multiplier, a not outlandish number that kept me in the stock after a near 50% rise from its March 2020 low. Facebook is cheaper than Amazon on my operating cash flow projections.

The armchair investor should appreciate that operating earnings mo-

mentum drives growth stocks. It's worth putting quarterly reports on your iPad to keep a feel for what you own. Facebook is selling on my estimate of free cash flow of $30 billion at over a 4% free cash flow. Believe this and it's a clincher, making the stock a strong hold. Facebook's premium over book value is seven times, but I never heard of anyone selling a growth stock based on its premium over book value. **You don't have to hold a card as a certified financial analyst to perform broad brush strokes on growth stocks and come up with the right answers.**

Sadly, corporate financial reports, both Amazon and Facebook, are cavalier, actually disgraceful, because they offer no color or details on research priorities, what tens of thousands of new employees will be working on or the competitive forces impacting them operationally. Financial report readers are offered a couple of dozen pages filled with comparative numbers, this year vs. last year. Hey guys, what happened to serious commentary? Am I the only one complaining?

Ironically, Warren Buffett believes that small investors should put their money in an index fund. Namely, the S&P 500 Index offering low-cost, long-term opportunity, having compounded over the decades at 7% adjusted for inflation. Stock picking is too difficult a job for the man in the Street.

A touch of irony rests in Buffett's own schema, which is compression of investments, not diversification. What went wrong for Berkshire Hathaway past decade, particularly past five years, was underperformance in bank stocks, specifically, and the value index bested by growth. Buffett missed the mushrooming of Internet and e-commerce paper like Amazon, Facebook, Alphabet, as well as Microsoft. He came late to Apple, but not too late to capture good relative performance therein.

Excitement over growth stocks dates back to the fifties when Polaroid's "instant" photography blossomed. The Dreyfus Fund's reputation was based on its concentrated PRD holding. The sixties belonged to major players in transistors and computers, namely, IBM, Texas Instruments, Motorola, Fairchild Camera and RCA in color television. Haloid Xerox traded OTC. In the background, a bunch of old guys followed U.S. Steel, General Motors and Standard Oil of New Jersey, but they didn't matter and shuffled off to oblivion.

Peak growth stock repute got memorialized in Morgan Guaranty's 1972 portfolio, where even Sears, Roebuck sold at 30 times earnings. Growth stocks sold at 2.7 times valuation of the S&P 500 Index.

Morgan Guaranty's Portfolio Largest Holdings

(Yearend, 1972)

Company	Price-Earnings Ratio	Premium Over Market Index
IBM	37.4	100%
Eastman Kodak	48.2	165%
Avon Products	65.1	253%
Sears, Roebuck	29.5	60%
Xerox	48.9	186%
Procter & Gamble	32.0	73%
Walt Disney	81.5	343%
Polaroid	90.7	393%
Schlumberger	57.2	211%

Each succeeding market cycle witnessed declining relative prices for growthies until the late nineties, when growth bottomed at parity with the S&P 500. Next stop, Coca-Cola and Microsoft sold at 1.5 times the market. Then NASDAQ took off for its 1998–1999 spring to 5,000. Lest we forget, there was an internet infrastructure family of companies that were total wipeouts after the tech bubble peaked in 2000. I don't even recall names like Akamai, Digital Island, Equinix, Exodus, Inktomi, Universal Access and Metromedia Fiber Network. All faded away.

Train to Outslug the Market

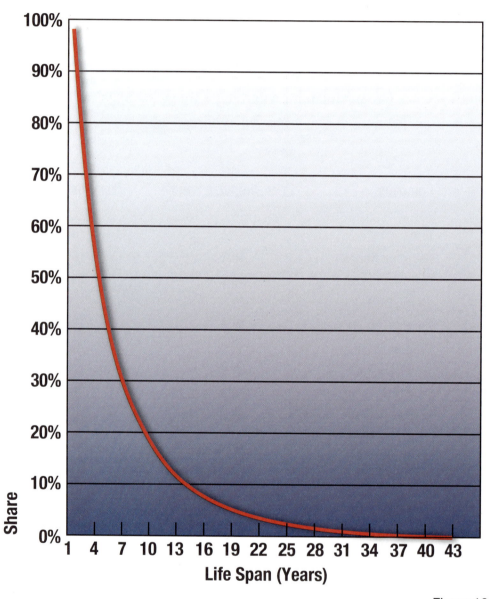

Figure 12
Source: Bernstein analysis.

Internet and e-Commerce Paper: Shadow Boxing in the Dark

The graph above on growth stock persistency is a sobering image for its players. Nothing is forever. You rarely get more than five years from your ponies. Marrying growth stocks for life can be dangerous, but past five years for internet and e-commerce stocks took many of us to the moon. GDP kinda paper like Exxon Mobil, General Motors, U.S. Steel and Alcoa became also-rans. Some even broke down into single digits.

15

Junk Bonds Worth Their Weight in Gold

It happens that certain material appears in the dream-content which cannot be subsequently recognized, in the waking state, as being part of one's knowledge and experience.
—Sigmund Freud, *The Interpretation of Dreams*

Diamonds should no longer be a girl's best friend. I'd exchange rocks, which yield zilch, for BB debentures yielding 5% or more. Basic to the valuation structure for everything in the world is the "cost of carry." I remember paying 7.5% for deal money in the eighties. Today I finance high-yield investments for 1% or next to nothing.

Calling a bond junk ain't descriptive enough. Five-year Treasuries now yield 25 basis points, down from 1.4% beginning of year. The spread between BB debentures with five-year duration is at 5%. Anyone owning five-year Treasuries should switch some capital herein.

My experience with junk goes far back, before Mike Milken, late fifties. My brother George was a major dealer in real junk. Dealers were tied in with teletype machines, but nobody discussed junk. It was mainly about spare parts.

If you wanted a rear bumper for a 1962-model Cadillac sedan, you called the local junk dealer. If he didn't inventory it, he'd get on his teletype and find one for you, somewhere in the country. Like trading high-yield paper, this was a spread business. After 40 years, my brother George found his junkyard situated

Junk Bonds Worth Their Weight in Gold

in the heart of Chico, California. Unplanned, Junky George found himself in the real estate business. Junk became a sideline.

Shouldn't we retire the "junk bond" sobriquet for high-yielding debentures? Despite dire warnings by Street pundits that this paper would succumb in the COVID-19 environment of deep recession, nothing bad has happened. Actually, my industrial pets thrive, hardly wobbling even in the darkest days of fear, March of 2020.

If you want to know what's junk, take a look at interest coverage for municipal bonds. It's nonexistent for many states and cities, now wards of White House largesse. Sans massive injections of federal liquidity, they'd succumb. Soaking the rich doesn't work, either. We'll move to tax-free states like Florida.

In the sixties, I remember visiting Sidney Homer, a senior Salomon Brothers partner whose book on the history of interest rates is a must-read. It covers 5,000 years. What happened when the wheat crop failed in Egypt in biblical times reminds me of the bread riots in Paris, 1789, when prices doubled.

Sidney's office perimeter was decked with charts showing monthly changes in spreads for Treasuries and corporates. Any violent swing called for a trading decision. Not that Solly's traders religiously listened to Sidney or to their economists like Henry Kaufman, whose annual study on the supply and demand for funds was a must-read for all of us. Nobody does this anymore.

Enormous swings in sentiment for even Baa-rated bonds show how crazily corporates do trade during a business cycle. When real GDP is shuffling along between 3% and 4%, such bonds can trade as low as a 150 basis-point premium to 10-year Treasuries. If bond players sniff recession in the air, premiums widen to as much as 350 basis points, almost overnight.

During the financial market meltdown of 2008–'09, yield premiums spiked to 650 basis points. Hysteria is built into the corporate-debenture market. Even in the tech-bubble-induced recession of 2001, yield premiums on Baa corporates zipped up from 150 to 350 basis points and then declined steadily for the next five years. All this happened while 10-year Treasury yields ticked at 2.2%

Train to Outslug the Market

with the Fed Funds rate a minimal 25 basis points.

Typically, Fed Funds historically average closer to 4%, not the next-to-zero rate we've seen. Nobody saw much tightening coming. If it does, professional panics in the bond crowd do get compressed into a couple of months. When I looked at a 30-year chart on Fed Funds, I was surprised to see a trendline closer to 6% when the economy was in a growthie condition. In a weakening state, junk bond yields can range easily between 500 and 700 basis points above five-year Treasuries. That's a panic yield worth consideration, particularly if you feel more deflation is in the air.

You'll never like quotes dealers give you on high-yield paper, going in or coming out. I tell them I don't mind being taken for quarters and halves, but if they press for full points, I'll stomp onto their trading floor and curse them out.

Rates on Black Monday, October 1987, yielded over 7%. Not even the tech-bubble collapse of 2000 induced rates lower than 5%. A chart on 10-year Treasuries mimics the chart on 30-year maturities. Rates broke below 5% finally in 2007 and progressed steadily lower.

Preferreds haven't participated in the bull market for Treasuries and corporates. My experience with them is they can be toxic. At the bottom of the financial meltdown in 2008–'09, Bank of America's preferred issue sold down to five bucks. Then it rallied when they arranged a multibillion-dollar capital infusion from Buffett's Berkshire Hathaway. Buffett made several billion on warrants issued to him in the financing terms.

I'd rate preferred stocks as single-B credits because the underlying properties are leveraged banks and insurance underwriters. For me, it's better to own single-B corporates yielding near 6% that aren't callable for seven to 10 years. In a low interest-rate setting they can rally 10% above par. Because I can do the security analysis on such companies, I feel comfortable. But, if you see recession around the corner, this paper can slide 10% practically overnight. The capacity for the bond market to panic—in both directions—is a seldom-mentioned phenomenon.

My portfolio positions that rallied with the stock market, early June 2020:

- **DISH**   7 3/4% of 7/1/21   @$110
- **Ford Motor**   6 5/8% of 10/1/28   @$100
- **HCA Healthcare**   5 3/8% of 9/1/26   @$110
- **Netflix**   5 7/8% of 11/15/28   @$116
- **Teva Pharmaceuticals**   6 3/4% of 2/1/28   @$111

I'm comfortable with the fundamentals for these bonds, but if the pandemic worsened, Ford Motor is the wrong place to invest. BB-rated corporates delivered 14% in 2014, the top return for all U.S. asset categories excepting the NASDAQ-100 Index. It could repeat in a slow growth setting, like 2020.

I learned to do all the work, but then follow my gut feel. What I liked in 2020 was in one sense I was arbitraging money, borrowing near a 1% rate. Owning stocks like AT&T and Exxon Mobil may not work out, even with 7% yields or more, if fundamentals don't improve. Corporate-debenture yields key off 10-year Treasuries in a benign setting.

I can't dredge up an economic cycle when interest rates for Treasuries and AAA corporates yield so little. Nothing under a 4% yield gets my money, ever, because my memory is so long, dating back to the fifties when stocks yielded more than bonds because stocks were deemed inferior in quality. Stocks yielding 5% were commonplace then, not only utilities but industrials, too. My parents loved U.S. Steel, even General Motors and Royal Dutch Petroleum.

Mid-2020, corporations with credit ratings below single-A tapped the new issue market at a premium over 10-year Treasuries of under 300 basis points. Consider, 10-year Treasury paper yielded 0.6%, single-A credits like Duke Energy sold 10-year bonds with a 1.75% yield, maybe 90 basis points over one-year Treasuries. A surrealistic picture prevailed in credit markets, worldwide. Zero to minus interest rates prevailed in Japan, even Germany. Pension funds with new cash flow wouldn't meet their actuarial assumptions on future liabilities set at 4.5%. Money market rates here ticked at 0.2% along with two-year Treasuries, while 10-year paper edged lower to 0.58%.

30-YEAR TREASURY BOND YIELD

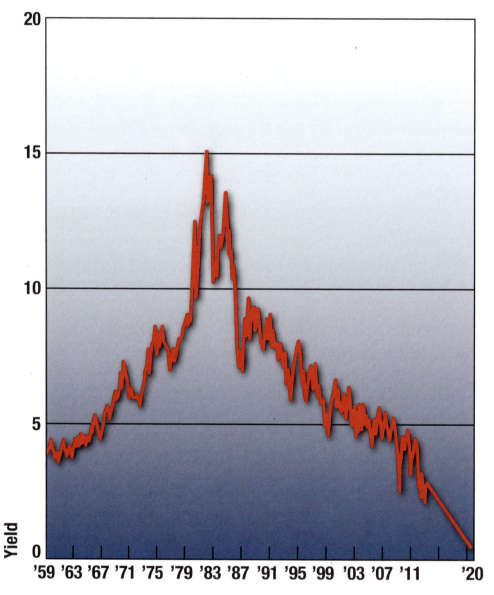

Figure 13
Source: Federal Reserve Board

This chart on 30-year Treasuries shows how the country emerged from its steady-position yield around 5% to much higher rates that reflected inflationary biases in the seventies when inflation bloomed. Treasuries sold to yield near 8%, tracking the rate of inflation. I was paying 7% for a billion-dollar bank-credit line with a 1% standby fee on top of it.

I'd focus on the real yield for 30-year Treasuries. This determines not only attractiveness of the stock market, but whether the bond market is playable. When such paper sticks below a real yield of 4%, the market multiplier does range as high as 18 times earnings, sometimes 20. What we had late 2020.

For bonds to see a real yield of 5%, much depends upon perception of the players. When inflationary numbers percolate, the market turns unattractive, just like early 2009. Most players were afraid of high-yield paper in 2020, anything below investment grade. But that's where yields of 6% dwelled. The fear of declining fixed-charges coverage moved to the foreground, unreasonably, unless COVID-19 persisted past 2020. Professional players had no edge over less-seasoned players, a condition I love to see happen, anytime, anywhere.

Today, our BB credits outside the energy sector are doing just fine. EBITDA coverage is improving. Many trade at $110 or higher. If you're not up 10% in high yields, something's wrong. In the tech bubble of 2000–2001, most internet stocks declined by 60% or more, but there were few defaults on bonds among bigger-capitalization houses.

Professional bond analysts, particularly in high yields, confine themselves to analyzing point spreads between various classes of bonds as to quality and maturity duration. For example, the current spread between 10-year Treasuries yielding 60 basis points and BB corporates yielding over 5% is historically enormous. Polite investors pass on high-yielding corporates. Fear in our COVID-19 world stayed pervasive.

I'd term many high-yield players a bunch of cowards who overreact during the business cycle. When U.S. real GDP plunges to zero or below, even the spreads between BAA bonds and U.S. Treasuries can widen from 150 basis points to 350. In the 2008–2009 meltdown, the spread spiked to over 550 basis points from its normalized trendline of 150 basis points.

With 10-year Treasuries yielding under 60 basis points, late 2020, the spread relative to BB paper approximates 440 basis points. So high-yield players stick agnostic on business-cycle recovery near at hand. Conversely, stock market operators since late March have fully discounted economic recovery, hopefully around the corner. How else explain our market selling near 20 times normalized earnings?

My conclusion is only prolonged recession impacts our so-called junk bonds. Consider, yields spiraled down relative to five-year Treasuries from 900 basis points to 300 basis points. The time period approximated three years, 2012 to 2015. Such downward volatility surprised me in its compacted intensity. It convinced me that buying into such extreme-downside volatility is the contrary course to follow.

Then, I looked at my chart on oil futures during this volatile period of 2008–2014. Financial meltdown, 2008–2009, oil futures followed the same downside trajectory as bank stocks, from $140 to $30 a barrel in 2009, comparably lethal. It reinforced my point of view that the spread between BB debentures and 5- and 10-year Treasuries favors BB paper, both as an absolute yield over 5% and a comfortable spread, historically speaking, with Treasuries and other volatile properties.

We may see zero to negative yields not just on money market paper but in Treasuries stretching out to five years. If so, my high-yield debentures with average duration of five years turn golden. Conversely, anyone investing in Treasuries today not only receives a next-to-nothing yield, but probably faces more downside risk than in BB paper.

The history in 10-year Treasury yields going back 60 years shows a trendline approximating 5%. Only the financial market's meltdown over 2008–2009 finally took yields down convincingly below 5%. Now we're flirting with a zero rate of return.

I am arbitraging my cost of borrowing against 5% yielders. Taking quality risk rather than duration risk is my preference. After all, our markets—equities, commodities and bonds—trace a volatile history going back to early postwar years.

In the sixties, Mike Milken was labeled by the financial press as the "Junk Bond King." Inaccurate, an oversimplification. Mike was an avid investment banker, thirsting to do deals. Antiestablishment operators who concocted take-over targets—Nelson Peltz, Meshulam Riklis, Carl Icahn, Ron Perelman, even Rupert Murdoch and John Kluge—came to Mike's unmarked door in Beverly Hills for their "Chinese money."

Establishment investment bankers refused to finance "hostiles." Ditto for Establishment banks like JPMorgan. Mike, through Drexel Burnham, raised capital for his honchos by selling high-yield paper to clients and the public. The democratization of capital raises on the Street became a noisy happening and a nightmare for the Establishment.

Ironically, Drexel Burnham destroyed itself when their cost-of-carry on high-yield bond inventory far exceeded portfolio yield. For players today, cost-of-carry is minimal, under 1%. So why isn't deal activity bubbling over? Because markets are pricey for most big-capitalization properties. Then, add on control premium.

Currently, under-$10 paper like General Electric, Ford Motor, U.S. Steel and sundry ragamuffins stands nearly overwhelmed by balance-sheet debt. Nobody's coming for them. What once was a spicy broth of deals spawning junk bond issuance, today is a ritual of comparing historical basis-point spreads. Underwritings key off 10-year to 30-year Treasuries, depending on the bond's stated maturity dating. Markets are referenced by historical yield curves, not the cast of characters thirsting for deal money.

In the seventies and eighties, junk bonds with warrants attached were the preferred deal weapons. I'll never forget my buddy Saul Steinberg emoting he wanted to take over Chemical Bank. Saul was maybe 27 years old and later settled for the Reliance Insurance property.

By the eighties, many old-line Wall Street houses had created their own operating divisions to enact hostile takeovers. Major banks participated in loans

Train to Outslug the Market

and credit lines ranging into billions. The air was filled with deal talk. Then, Black Monday (October 1987) hit the Street and deal money dried up. Value investors like Larry Tisch and Warren Buffett got busy buying stocks that had declined 25%, overnight.

Nowadays, the high-yield market is tapped by old-line bleeding corporations operating cash flow negative. American Airlines, Boeing, oil operators, hotels, casinos and retail chains. Operators like Carl Icahn threaten proxy solicitations to gain control and use their home capital as the earnest stake.

Alas, mid-2020, I violated my discipline, buying a newly underwritten American Airlines convertible debenture with a 6% coupon. At least, I bought it at $95 a day after issue and the conversion premium wasn't excessive (maybe?). Weeks later, this dog traded in the low eighties, but I brushed this off. After all, I bought Bank of America's preferred at $5 in 2009.

No Nifty Fifty— Pick Half a Dozen

Until now, there's no period in financial history when a half-dozen mega caps waxed so dominant. Trillion-dollar capitalizations like Microsoft, Apple and Amazon are followed by Facebook and Alphabet. Then, throw in Alibaba, not a Big Board stock. This half dozen tots up to over a $5 trillion valuation. As a frame of reference, GDP is a $30 trillion number.

Earnings surprises, both up and down, happen quarterly. The Street rarely gets its numbers right because management's guidance is minimal. Quarterly reports are in stats comparing year-over-year results. Market volatility is twice that of the S&P 500 Index. In short, they're destined to lead the market on the way up, and coming down, they do cave in.

Going back to the 1972 Nifty Fifty portfolio of Morgan Guaranty Trust, you'd find gross overvaluation, but many of the names were analyzable. Amazon is unanalyzable, unlike IBM, Eastman Kodak, Avon Products, Sears, Roebuck, Xerox, Procter & Gamble, Walt Disney, Schlumberger and Polaroid. Premiums over the market ranged from 100% for IBM to over 300% for Polaroid and Walt Disney. Nobody blinked or called the king naked.

These babies, called one-decision stocks by their advocates, were bought and held, never sold. Analyst jockeys told their clients to expect appreciation to compound 2%, monthly. The analogy with internet and e-commerce paper today runs scary with comparable awe and reverence that disregards conventional valuation yardsticks. Nobody can sharp-pencil Amazon or Tesla today or, 50 years ago, Polaroid, which still sold at 90 times earnings in 1978.

Train to Outslug the Market

Edwin Land would preside at his annual meeting in a Boston park setting. He'd hold up his new products and declaim how everyone in the world would carry the new Swinger camera on his shoulder. Steve Jobs copied Land in his presentation format to Apple's shareholders with good results.

As money managers today, maybe we'll get away with such bucolic optimism for a couple more years. For me, the mid-2020 market was precariously perched. I stood 50% in equities but, volatility adjusted, maybe 75%.

So much has changed. Back in 2001, General Electric held the numero uno post position with a market capitalization of $416 billion; mid-2020, just at $75 billion. Microsoft then was at $300 billion, the follow-up placement. Twenty years ago, IBM and Intel made the top 10, which included two drug houses, Merck and Pfizer. Then, JPMorgan Chase, Citigroup and Wells Fargo made it into top 25 listing. Exxon Mobil filled the number three slot at $282 billion.

Consider, Exxon Mobil went through all the motions of being a world player in energy, but nearly 20 years later their market cap is not much above $200 billion. Even four years ago, Apple, Microsoft and Exxon held the top three slots, with Berkshire Hathaway, a proxy for bank stocks, then number five.

Stocks like General Electric and General Motors today are irrelevant. I was shocked to see market caps of Alcoa and U.S. Steel trading for petty cash, sporting $5 billion valuations. Netflix, with a market cap of $160 billion, gets as much press coverage as Amazon or Facebook. Pricey industrials like Boeing were cut in half while a major bank like Citigroup showed amplitude of price over 12 months from over $80 to under $40.

Timing your entry level for a new position is half the battle for investment primacy. I've ignored non-durable properties like Coca-Cola and exclude most drug houses as fully priced. You're paying too much to be immune to the business cycle. Conversely, basic industrials mid-2020 are too pricey at 18 to 20 times forward 12-months projections.

Seldom remarked, disbelief in growth surfaced in 2013–'14. Then, gross margins for tech traced a downward pattern—a key leading indicator. The market traded at 17 times earnings in 2014. Currently, it's the packagers of entertainment, information and telecommunications that are leveraging technology. These are now household names: Apple, Alphabet, Comcast, Netflix, Facebook and Amazon. Because of high valuation, these stocks are gut plays, caught in the push-pull of how long their numbers can go on and on. Don't ask what I owned 50 years ago. Certainly, Polaroid and Xerox, but I was early and did say "bye-bye."

Our research floor at EF Hutton got the first 914 copier on Wall Street because our chemicals analyst, Ralph Reis, knew Kent Damon, Xerox's chief financial officer. Suddenly, secretaries from all floors made tracks to the 914 for copies of their work. Ralph and I slipped our slide rules to extrapolate Xerox's revenues. They were extraordinary and we were early. Xerox still had Haloid as part of its name, later dropped. It was analyzed by chemicals specialists.

I couldn't deal with Amazon after its double to $3,000. If Amazon's revenues come in up 19% for the quarter instead of analysts' consensus of 21%, the stock would drop a snappy 10%, overnight. This is loony tunes but expresses the market's instability. We see this not only in Amazon, but periodically in Facebook, Alphabet and Microsoft. Oil majors like Exxon Mobil and polite financials like American Express and JPMorgan Chase do swoon up to 20% or more in a couple of months, not years.

The 40-year trend line for price-earnings ratios is 15, not 18 to 20 times posted numbers. The exception was the 2000–'01 tech bubble when insanity pushed by outlandish analytical yardsticks, like multiples of revenues, led to a psychotic market. A year later, full payback. It took over a decade for NASDAQ to recover. Disbelief in growth surfaced again in 2013–'14 when stocks like Apple, Microsoft and Cisco Systems sold at discounts to stock market valuation. The premium for Google (Alphabet) was just 10%, same as Coca-Cola. That's when you're supposed to come to the plate and take a swat.

Why so many bargains then? Chalk it up to negative earnings surprises. Gross operating margins for tech houses traced a downward slope. Midyear, nobody, including me, is projecting a downward slope in tech operating margins. They look pretty solid but valuation is heady, even using enterprise value rather than earnings as your basic metric.

If you believe in some discount for excessive options issuance (over 20% of revenues), it's difficult to rationalize big-cap tech houses, like Salesforce.com. Microsoft started aggressive options award methodology going back to 1986. Usage by the internet houses got out of hand. The SEC has never taken a stand on the non-GAAP earnings report methodology. I believe, like Warren Buffett, it's a recurring expense and should be debited as such by the market.

All this reminds me why quality California Cabernet has become so pricey. Not because vintages now are far superior to, say, 1975. It's because the price of wine grape-growing land soared from $7,500 an acre to $750,000 currently. So, the cost of doing business is exponentially higher, but has topped out now, and winemakers' results are headed down. I was offered a vineyard in 1975, but turned it down as too pricey. Failed to construe that I wasn't buying a wine-maker, but rather grape acreage. Quality cabernet then sold at $20 a bottle, not $150, today's level.

Same goes for costs of attracting computer engineering talent to Silicon Valley. It should be reflected in lower rather than higher price-earnings val-uations for internet and e-commerce operators. So far, the Street ignores this issue. My critical metric for valuation in tech focuses on operating cash flow. This earthy number shows wherewithal that management holds to work with to grow their footprint. Keeps me attached to Facebook.

Without a sense of historic valuation, don't even dream of becoming a contrarian. Prices for basic industrials and materials stocks like Alcoa, U.S. Steel, Ford Motor, General Motors, even DuPont de Nemours and Boeing show 12-month amplitude ranging up to 50%. Boeing dropped like a stone when one of its new model 737s crashed into the sea. A new altitude sensor bore some responsibility. From $390 to below par. Boeing is a plaything, for me, not investable.

The market swings on a handful of stocks. Scroll past top-five names and individual weightings drop to 1.5% positions or lower. JPMorgan Chase, John-son & Johnson, Exxon Mobil and AT&T have been around practically forever.

No Nifty Fifty—Pick Half a Dozen

The likes of Microsoft, Amazon, Apple, Facebook, Alphabet and Berkshire Hathaway approach 20% of index weighting. Develop a point of view here or don't consider yourself a player.

Berkshire Hathaway radiates the power of compounding good stock picking over 60 years. The other five demonstrate the magic of technological leverage, which foreshortens the time it takes for companies to emerge as mega caps. Amazon is the sole name I can think of that became numero uno on revenue growth, not earnings power on e-commerce revenues. We're in mid-story here, my fingers crossed.

Disbelief in Growth Surfaced in 2013–2014

Company	Estimated Premium or Discount to Stock Market Valuation – May 2014
Google	10%
Apple	-10%
Merck	zero
Eli Lilly	zero
Bristol-Myers Squibb	zero
PepsiCo	+15%
Hewlett-Packard	-35%
Proctor & Gamble	zero
Coca-Cola	10%
Intel	10%
Microsoft	-10%
McDonald's	zero
Cisco Systems	-20%
Oracle	-15%

Train to Outslug the Market

By sector, financials are weightier than energy and health care. Boeing remains a lonely growth industrial. This says a lot about the locus of the country, namely technology and financials, not Ford and Exxon, which date back over a century. Think about your portfolio in such terms. You may be obsolete, an incurable collector with dead paper in hand. Sears, Roebuck won't renew itself. Polaroid is gone, while Xerox hangs in as a low-priced conglomerate, a failure in its diversification efforts.

Who holds staying power today? Good question, I ask myself, periodically. Citigroup, depths of the 2008–'09 meltdown, traded near zero, practically a ward of the state. It now ticks around $80, but the high, set late 2006, could stand forever, namely, $570, adjusted for the reverse stock split years ago. This table on the compression of price-earnings ratios is a reminder that at times "growth" is a dirty word.

Actually, during the sixties, the market stayed keen on growth stocks, which sold at 60 times earnings. The Street rationalized such insanity as "scarcity value." Walter Annenberg then indulged himself in Picasso canvases after he sold *TV Guide* to Rupert Murdoch at a growth-stock price point.

The conceit in tripping to the moon on a handful of stocks need not be reserved for a handful of operators, like Carl Icahn, Warren Buffett and Bill Ackman. **Nobody holds a monopoly on brains.** All armchair investors need to do is creep into the head of the Federal Reserve Board chairman who mid-2020 was panic-stricken by the COVID-19 pandemic. Interest rates stay next to zero for the foreseeable future. You can project any inflation coming or GDP momentum as good as he can. Same goes for price-earnings ratios in a normal setting.

The herd instinct to retain the money management arm of JPMorgan and its ilk is all wrong. The pie-chart construct of 60% equities, 40% bonds only works if you're in growth stocks and high-yield debentures. These so-called institutional managers hardly ever give any weighting to the NASDAQ-100 Index, which midyear 2020 is outperforming the other indices. And, why not?

HOW TO STAY OUT OF TROUBLE:

- Never buy into anything that sells at over two times its growth rate.
- If management's compensation is outlandish, pass them by.
- Read proxy statements, even if they're 80 pages long. If disparity between GAAP and non-GAAP earnings is over 20%, don't play.
- If management acts unethically, pass or sell out your position. Let management be tough but fair.
- There are compromises to be made. Mark Zuckerberg and Facebook still draw a terrible press, but Facebook's numbers speak louder. I'm unhappy that they tell you practically nothing, spend billions on R&D, but don't amplify on priority projects.
- Not that Jeff Bezos tells you much, either. Bezos treats the analyst fraternity like kindergartners in terms of guidance. Analysts, like economists, rarely catch inflection points.
- Look for pivotal macros like technology capital spending. It triggered the 2015 recovery. In Facebook's case, the level of advertising spending is a coincidental indicator. Your guess on the economy is as good as theirs.

17

Entry Points Count

Intraday volatility for stocks, whether $10 numbers or growthies selling in three digits, can range between 5% and 10%. You see such action in U.S. Steel, Alcoa, Energy Transfer, General Electric and Ford Motor—all under-$10 paper, but with few friends. Meanwhile, Facebook, Amazon, Tesla, even Microsoft, Nvidia and Netflix prove equally volatile, leading the market up or downside.

You'd expect such action in our damaged setting. Sitting above ragamuffins in the $10–$20 range are companies like Teva Pharmaceuticals, Occidental Petroleum, Schlumberger, Freeport-McMoRan, Williams Partners, Alcoa and Halliburton. All equally explosive, both ways.

Players competing are day traders, mathematicians using sentiment algorithms as well as money managers buying or selling volatility. They're disinterested in long-term fundamentals on specific properties. Holding periods could run as short as a couple of minutes. Day trading is for a 19-year-old who thirsts to conquer the world, but fails miserably.

Rarely is anything celebratory going on intraday. Don't expect to see George Washington coming down to Wall Street mounted on his nearly white horse, Blueskin. I remember Citigroup trading near a buck a share in 2009, before they managed a reverse split to get their stock respectably trading in the low teens. This is comparable with Chesapeake Energy's reverse split, done on the doorstep of its bankruptcy, June 2020.

I hold no illusions about what I own. A bad quarter takes down Microsoft a snappy 10% or more, overnight. There's always liquidity, but at a price you may not like. Michael Milken made a market in practically everything under the sun. I was a better buyer than seller, picking up huge blocks of Caesars World, the New York Times and Geico when there were more block sellers than buyers.

The working phrase is "stocks can sell anywhere," up or down. I can't explain Tesla, ticking over $1,500, or even Amazon at $2,600. More easily, I understand why an overleveraged property like Occidental Petroleum did collapse. Leverage is the killer. I bought Halliburton at $7 because I thought they could carry their debt through a negative scenario for oil demand, worldwide. A year earlier, Halliburton ticked at $29.

Welcome darkest-before-dawn kind of plays that include Energy Transfer, Williams and Teva but not General Electric, Ford, Macy's, U.S. Steel and Alcoa. Here, balance-sheet analysis prevails, not the income statement. Try to convince yourself that the property under the microscope has wherewithal to sustain at least two years of cyclical downside.

You pay and pay if entry points are too high. Consider major reserve city banks like Citigroup, Bank of America and Wells Fargo; even JPMorgan Chase dropped 40% from highs in December 2019. According to Wall Street, the industry outlook was positive. Interest rates were headed up and margins on loans would soar. A tightly construed analysis, but 100% wrong. Timing is everything. Come in on top of a universally bullish consensus for an industry or stock, and probably it's too late to play.

Rather than use the word "timing," I call it "apperceptive mass," a point of view developed from experiencing half a dozen economic cycles and financial panics. When panic is in the streets, you're supposed to unleash buying power, unless you truly believe the world is coming to an end.

If you think COVID-19 is going to kill tens of millions, worldwide, the market has just begun a violent downward trajectory that will curl your hair. Similarly, if you believe there's too much industrial capacity in steel, oil, copper and aluminum, underlying stocks like U.S. Steel, Ford and leveraged oils like Occidental Petroleum end up unwanted basket cases. Same goes for many financial houses, banks and brokers. I bet on Lehman Brothers as a survivor in 2009, but I was wrong. Merrill Lynch disappeared into the maws of Bank of America. It was a once-proud operator over five decades.

Walmart, for example, is analyzed on forward 12-month operating margins and projected revenues. This is closer to bedrock reality. The business cycle can intervene, but hopefully, such potential variance is incorporated in its price-earnings ratio. I own Amazon, but passed on Walmart. Sounds crazy, but it's what money managers do. They pass on the obvious and buy into dreams depending on where you are in the country's business cycle and whether speculation is in the air or deflated.

Stock picking works or fails based on your working hypothesis for the business cycle and the proper price-earnings ratio for the market next 12 months. The entire wealth-management industry is structured around a 60/40 ratio of equities to fixed income investments. This thesis is dolled up by including dollops in offshore markets, commodities, oil futures and gold, even emerging-market debt.

Nobody ever suggests or implements an aggressive point of view that you should be double-weighted in the NASDAQ-100 Index (me, me, me) or concentrate in high-yield bonds, not Treasuries. By shunning passive implementation, poor performance relative to benchmarks is avoided. What I've seen of banks' institutional portfolios is they're underperforming by a percentage point or two. Their pie charts on investment strategies suggest to clients that they are activists, not asleep at the switch. Maybe yes, maybe no.

Here goes: I've 30% of assets in NASDAQ-100 kind of stocks like Microsoft, Facebook, Alibaba and Amazon. Another 30% rests in ragamuffins like Halliburton, Freeport-McMoRan, Teva, Williams, Energy Transfer and Enterprise Products Partners. Nobody can accuse me of not implementing a barbell strategy in stocks.

The high-yield bond market for me is a 40% position, in BB debentures averaging five years' duration. Fear of recession and consequently declining fixed-charges coverage still permeates in junk bonds. This is a serious construct

Entry Points Count

alternative to AAA credit-rated debt.

Would you rather own 10-year Treasuries yielding 74 basis points? Recent-years' history is against you. The spread between high-yield bonds and 10-year Treasuries is now 425 basis points, an attractive entry point for so-called junk.

The Innermost Game of Investing

Like a professional singer or musician, I like to tune up with scales and arpeggios. It gets me concentrated on the here and now and takes about 30 minutes of pre-opening "practice." What I'm trying to do is program myself to be a winner rather than play defensive ball. You can't invest like John McEnroe used to play tennis. Lose your temper and you'll pay dearly. Buying at tops, selling at bottoms, discarding winners and staying with losers are emotional gin-rummy kinds of decisions that turn out badly. Bernard Baruch summed it up when the anxious player handed him his portfolio and asked for advice, and without even looking at the list, Baruch just said, "Sell it down to your sleeping level."

Our traders canvas the Street for me. I know which houses are upgrading or downgrading stocks, changing earnings projections or publishing "think pieces" on the market, the economy, specific stock sectors or big-capitalization stocks that we follow. If the analysts or pundits are serious professionals, I'll ask for a printout and get it in minutes. By 8:30 a.m. I've caught up on the rest of the world's overnight statistics. I know where the continental bourses and the Nikkei averages have ticked, the price change in gold and oil, which currencies have rippled out of alignment. Many Department of Commerce monthly series statistical releases are published at 8:30, too. Consumer prices, unemployment, retail sales and changes in inventories are released. The bond market opens at 9:00 and takes its cue from these numbers, which the *Wall Street Journal* fashions into stories for its next-day edition.

The Innermost Game of Investing

By the time you've read the papers, the news is already discounted in the marketplace. Similarly, earnings releases and news on mergers, acquisitions and takeovers normally print on the tickers intraday. The news from the Capitol on the progress of specific legislative initiatives like health care, defense spending and budget issues are early-on leaks and comparably stale by the time you read it in your paper of record. I assume anything I read is at least two days old and the Street's players, both traders and money managers, have digested it long before the public sees it in print.

Nobody should spend more than 15 minutes on any newspaper. I digest the *Wall Street Journal*, *Financial Times* and the *New York Times*, including its sports section, in 30 minutes, over breakfast. The *Times* tells me about wars, national disasters and infighting in the Capitol. I find the *Financial Times* columnists less Establishment oriented. Their focus is the continent. When something is rotten at Daimler AG, they bring the story sharply into focus.

Before I open the *WSJ*, I scan the table of contents for stories of prospective investment significance or pieces that can embellish our scope on running policy initiatives like health care and the budget. On March 24, 2001, the New York Times published a front-page story that the Republicans were considering a $60 billion up-front tax cut. Because I believed the country needed upward of $300 billion, I concluded nobody in the Capitol was tuned in to the seriousness of the impending recession. It kept me from putting cash reserves to work with the market in a free-fall mode.

In the *WSJ*, turn to the box on "Most Active Issues," a list of 15 NYSE stocks. Sometimes, there's a discernible pattern that you store in your bank of apperceptive mass. Sector rotation within the market and specific industry groups falling in or out of favor are intermediate-term trends that you must process. I watch this list like I would a pinball machine lighting up and buzzing as the steel balls bounce off the rubbers.

For me, the most revealing daily stock table is the "new high" list. The *WSJ* and Times publish this box in the smallest type size known to the western world; the Times makes this crucial data practically invisible to the naked eye.

Train to Outslug the Market

By March of 2001, the new high list was all but obliterated, suggesting the market's breadth was narrowly based. You attack and dissect this list by carrying forward a couple of deep basics. **Most of your money needs to work in sectors that are acting better than the market. Your stocks should be big-capitalization properties with excellent liquidity and no serious financial risk.**

The daily new high list tells me which buses are leaving the station and compels me to reassess our major sector weightings. When a big-cap stock, over $100 billion, hits the list without me, I begin screaming for the full story in 24 hours or less with charts, tables, 10-Ks, analysts' reports, whatever it takes to make a decision, thumbs-up or thumbs-down.

To add scope and emphasis to the daily new high snapshot, I track big-capitalization stocks with outstanding monthly and year-to-date performance. These shooting stars confirm where the flow of new money is headed. You begin to see clear-cut patterns of sector strength and you sort out stocks for analytical coverage you normally pass on.

After all the snapshots are digested, you switch to a wide-angle lens for annual reports and 10-Ks, which frequently revise all that's gone on. Yearend write-offs, changes in accounting conventions for research, health care, pensions, depreciation and inventories are common for even hallowed names like IBM, General Motors and Procter & Gamble. Aside from outright fraud and embezzlement, I find 95 out of 100 annual reports worthless.

I lug home dozens. By midnight, I'm fast asleep, the carpet littered with the blue-suited carcasses of corporate chairmen, their messages in stilted corporatese, moribund and mute. The frequency of four-color photography and the size of the books vary directly with stock prices. It will take two Black Mondays, back to back, to squash annuals down to a sane 24-page production. Walmart did it in 20 pages. Their numbers speak louder than words on recycled paper.

Not only do you need to purge emotional reactions to losses, but to successful plays as well. **Never judge yourself as a good or bad investor. Your ego stays out of the business.** There are no good stocks or bad stocks. When a stock you buy turns south, ask yourself whether your entry point was timely or not.

The Innermost Game of Investing

If anxiety is fear of the future, concentrate on bringing action or reaction back to present time.

Financial information at the margin unfolds daily. Process it dispassionately. Ninety-five percent of what you hear and read is noise to be discarded as garbage. Maybe 5% of overnight news requires a follow-up to see whether it modifies your point of view on how the future will unfold for the world, the country, specific industries or companies. Close reading of quarterly corporate reports is a must.

Securities analysts, like Talmudic scholars, start at the back where the footnotes to the financials are printed in small type. When the headman's message opens with "Results for your company were mixed," you know your company is up to its waist in quicksand. An entire subsector of the public relations industry does nothing but design and write four-color jobs for hundreds of companies. Their diction and artwork are readily interchangeable.

If you read a dozen annual reports of banks yearend 2007, you would never have known their loan portfolios were crumbling into dust. Not even a hint of the fiasco in mortgage paper. This is the "One-Hoss Shay" kind of poetic license. Everything is growth, growth, growth, except every three or four years there's an enormous restructuring write-off. Everyone charges off billions for "restructuring initiatives." Wall Street analysts love write-offs because then they can go back to extrapolating growth for the next cycle. Everyone ignores the fact that the write-off engulfed and devoured years of previously reported earnings and net worth. Even IBM was guilty in its lean years.

Few annuals tell you what's ahead for the new year. The documents chronicle the past without interpreting dialectics of change. Distortion is comparable to looking through a rearview mirror. After x-ing out glossy photos, I look for nuances of change in the corporate mindset. Sometimes it's reassuring to find management is as tough as ever about getting its stock to dance.

Searching through IBM's wreckage, early nineties, I uncovered one last damning piece of evidence. The shareholders list rested intact! IBM still boasted three-quarters of a million owners despite its year-to-year $25 billion shrinkage

137

in market value. Inertia among investors, both institutional and individual, can never be underestimated. It suggests the public's image of IBM hadn't changed in 10 years—before Apple, Compaq, Dell and Sun Microsystems pecked 'em to death. I placed the IBM book cover-up on my worktable as a reminder that money management is a continuous process of reality testing. **A management that can't write a candid and organized report to shareholders is a company you don't want to own at any price—until they fess up.**

IBM finally changed. John Akers took early retirement and an outsider, Lou Gerstner, came in and cleansed the stables. Years later, a sailing buddy of Tom Watson explained it to me in two sentences. For years they had the business all to themselves. Watson built up layer upon layer of management and could never react fast enough to change. The 2000 IBM annual was a great read, full of info on how management was positioning its company for the years ahead. Intel and Cisco Systems needed to reinvent themselves by 2014, but nowhere could you find management pronouncing adequately on research priorities, capital investment and divestitures.

During the early sixties, as a securities analyst I had to disabuse the tailored partners I reported to on stocks they loved to recommend. Many lived in the past, their perception of the management and competitive mettle of companies like GM, International Paper and International Harvester sadly unfocused. In the nineties this myopia was even more dangerous considering the dimming future of Eastman Kodak, Xerox, Procter & Gamble, Motorola, Kellogg, Sears, Roebuck, Allstate and dozens more that were held in high esteem for too long.

I pore over hundreds of annuals, and maybe a handful hit pay dirt as actionable research ideas. Like a homicide detective interrogating a suspect, you listen to what is said or unsaid, read the body language, and squint at the small-print evidence. Finally, the symbolism emerges—they're either winners or losers. First read the footnotes in the back. Then, look at the disparity between GAAP and non-GAAP earnings. If it's more than 10%, chances are the company is being run for management and key employees.

For the do-it-yourself investor, accept my point of view that you can only invest wisely if you have sifted all the available facts in any situation. When you develop a macroeconomic point of view that diverges from the consensus, implement it aggressively. Assume that if you've hit the mark, the consensus will fall into line within six months. But actively monitor your working hypothesis. It has to be reconfirmed with unfolding statistical data.

Don't be stubborn. If the facts don't fit your conclusion, fold your hand. When the facts reconfirm your position, buy more. Finally, you plan an exit strategy based on a model of valuation that relates stock prices to their return on capital over a full cycle. The serious investor is ever sensitive to macro events and how they play out in industry sectors and subsectors like oil drillers. I'm always thinking about what's ahead for the next 12 months, but no more. You never get the variables right for long, no more than half the time, but it's better than nothing.

The reason for due diligence is to muster courage to act without inhibition, particularly when markets are hysterically ebullient or in a panic mode. I keep telling myself that the only reason to do security analysis is to muster conviction to buy the properties you know when they are in free fall. I did this with Citigroup, Bank of America, Sirius XM Radio, Goldman Sachs, Gilead Sciences, Boeing and Las Vegas Sands. Conversely, I couldn't buy into the technology rout in March of 2001, unable to benchmark properties like Cisco Systems, Intel and EMC. There was more than an inventory glut. Capital spending had dried up for their customers.

When you know an industry and all the players involved who manage the primary properties, as the sector segues into its cycle, you shed lingering reservations and swing for the fences. I did this in the gaming industry in the eighties when Vegas was still underbuilt but beginning to turn into a family destination resort. A great player of craps watched me for an hour and then chided me for playing defensively. You're supposed to play to win, taking the full odds behind the line whenever you can. My feeble excuse was that I was out of my element. Wall Street is where I'd learned to be fearless, to separate the real from the unreal, to leverage institutional stupidity and time my buying into panics just when dawn was about to break.

I did this better when I was younger and had much less to lose. When Roger Blough of U.S. Steel faced off with President Kennedy over raising steel prices, the Street panicked, anticipating price controls. But Jack Kennedy was counseled by his father, Joe Kennedy, a seasoned corporate player, who advised his son to cool his jets. I bought Xerox, fully margined in 1962, and it worked.

In 1961, the Cuban Missile Crisis put the country and the USSR on the eve of launching nuclear missiles. I stepped back from watching this unfold and said to myself if the Russians allow Castro to arm and launch his medium-range missiles, it's all over for everyone. I wasn't living in Toronto, so I bet that either party would back down. I won. I remember the tape running five to six hours late, and the executions for all the growth stocks I had filled out buy-slips for came in the next morning. That evening, I walked across the Brooklyn Bridge to my apartment in Brooklyn Heights, content and rich. Next morning, the head of margin credit at my house scolded me for exceeding my buying power. I had to be punished. No margin for 30 days. I miss old Wall Street!

I did take an academic interest in Cuba. Thirty years later I learned that Castro was screaming at the Russian advisors in Cuba to launch the targeted missiles to our mainland but the Russians refused. The world came within an inch of obliteration. I got lucky, but I had programmed myself to win, concentrated on the here and now in space and time. If I had bet this way on the eve of World War I, that the major powers would finally turn rational, I would have lost everything in the summer of 1914.

Positive federal dynamics got me back into the market early in 2009. The Troubled Asset Relief Program (TARP) devised by Geithner and Bernanke bailed out Citigroup, General Motors, American International Group, Bank of America and Fanny Mae and Freddie Mac. Stocks had touched down at 10 times earnings, yielding over 5%. Historically this is deep valuation territory that sucks in value players.

Unlike many of my generation, I've eschewed short selling because it screws

The Innermost Game of Investing

up my head and makes me anxious. I do write covered calls against long positions when the market feels toppy. Sometimes, I'll box positions by selling calls and using the proceeds to buy puts. Again, all this activity is aimed at quieting the mind to reconcentrate on maximizing bull-market plays.

In America, at least in the long run, optimism pays. The stock market has outperformed all other assets despite its blackish Mondays. Staying invested is more fruitful than moving into and out of markets, particularly if you're running billions. I've learned not to forecast too definitively on interest rates and the valuation structure of the market. It's better to seek out companies, businesses, industries and management that you believe are going into phase and stay with them for five years, sometimes longer. Finally, never fall in love with a stock that goes up and makes you feel smart, like the old Xerox. You'll regret it.

If you need more love and admiration, buy a dog. My wife and I lived with 10 poodles. Six standards and four toys. We bred and exhibited same.

Don't ever do too much fine tuning. Over 35 years, the market was driven to despair, below 10 times earnings in 1982, and to euphoria, 25 times in pre–tech bubble 2000. The ultimate valuation buy point came in the spring of 2009 when our government saved the financial system, then at 10 times earnings, from its supreme and broad-based stupidity and bold greed. Greed is not always good, carried to excess, pussycats.

Mid-2020, the COVID-19 pandemic took on renewed force. Too many states had lifted restrictions prematurely on movement and gathering places. I didn't feel as yet the worst was over or even near at hand. The S&P 500 broiled around 3,200, fully discounting the next few years' recovery dimensions. I stayed at 60% invested largely in tech houses and in rank-recovery speculations like Halliburton and Freeport-McMoRan. I felt the only edge I had was my courage, but maybe it wasn't enough.

30-YEAR S&P 500 INDEX VALUATION RANGE

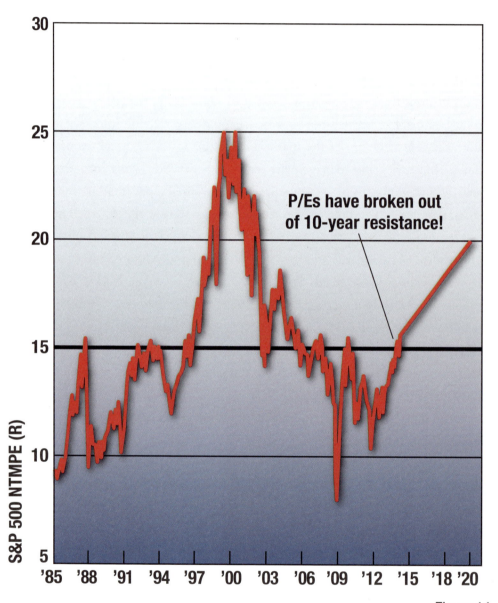

Figure 14

19

Flee Grandiosity, the Killer White Whale

World Trade Center, NY, Joseph Sohm © Shutterstock

I was always attracted to frugal operators like Larry Tisch, who busily bought up supertankers then scrapped by Exxon and other oil majors. Larry was standing on the deck of a 200-meter leviathan. "You mean you get all this for a million bucks?" he asked. Maybe, big oil is headed to its scrap value, fully discounting reserves in the ground. The SEC needs to step in here on full disclosure.

What would Alexander Hamilton think of today's electronic trading or the Federal Reserve Board's buying low-rated corporate bonds? Even Renaissance Technologies, the computer-driven asset house managing $75 billion, couldn't handle the market's intraday volatility in the spring of 2020. They were down 20%, dozens of their mathematicians nonplussed.

Ironically, a repeat of Black Monday could happen because of panic selling rather than overspeculation. Lest we forget, in the 2008–'09 meltdown, Lehman Brothers, Bear Stearns, even Merrill Lynch stood overleveraged in unsalable real estate and junk bonds during the period of interest rates running up to 8%. The cost-of-carry for leveraged assets exceeded their yield, a killer situation.

I worry about unintended consequences of sucking in a new generation of buyers for mutual funds, ETFs and indexed paper. Trillions in equities are held passively and someday may approach the equivalent of GDP.

Chuck Schwab's near-zero commissions rate structure turned Schwab into one gigantic play on interest rates. They arbitrage client credit balances, paying out much less than they earn on reinvestment. Schwab, in short, is a money market fund parading as a full-fledged brokerage house. When I sniff a steeper yield curve coming, Schwab becomes playable.

I'm awed by the immensity of the financial world these days. BlackRock and others control trillions in exchange-traded funds and mutual funds. This awesome boodle has doubled in size past five years. Late fifties, when I subwayed down to Wall Street, it was a small village with a heavy-glass ceiling. Women solely populated the typists' pool. Female analysts were rare, deemed too emotional to manage money. A WASP conclave presided, quietly, in place. They traded mainly in Treasuries and AAA debentures, not in equities. Partners didn't arrive at work until 10:00 a.m., after the market's opening bell. They were well-tailored anachronisms.

A few years later, Mickie Siebert, a standout female operator, fought for and won a seat on the New York Stock Exchange. The Street, finally, was turning into a meritocracy. When Bell Laboratories' invention of the semiconductor was licensed to all comers, technology took off as a burgeoning sector in the S&P 500 Index. Now it's over a 25% weighting, up from 3% in 1960.

Late fifties, money managers like Jerry Tsai and Leon Levy of Oppenheimer stepped into the empty spotlight. George Soros was running a $20 million hedge fund, which was considered a lot of money then. The public had no idea that hedge funds existed or how they operated.

Brokerage commissions, early sixties, stood outrageously high, and that was accepted as the norm. A round lot (100 shares) at $50 carried a $50 commission, 1% of principle. A decade later, the SEC instituted negotiated rates, which drove boutique research houses out of business. Nobody understood how low commissions would transform the Street and broaden public participation.

Elsewhere, grandiosity is expressed in 90-story condominiums and office buildings now troubled by rent softening and rising vacancies. Fortunately, the cost-of-carry is lower in this cycle than in 1973–'74, a bloody downcycle. You coulda bought half of Park Avenue for a song in 1973. I was considered a nut job for buying an apartment in the Dakota for $87,500.

Consider, the World Trade Center, a case of political grandiosity, was the brainchild of Nelson Rockefeller. The 9/11 tragedy need not have happened in the Big Apple. The buildings never should have seen daylight. Rockefeller prevailed on the board of the Port Authority of New York and New Jersey to sop up their excess capital in this project. It remained under-occupied, depressing downtown office rents for a decade.

New York's Metropolitan Transit Authority utilized the New York subway system as their private piggy bank. Bloated salaries proliferated amid neglected maintenance. It could cost New York tens of billions to set things right. In my time, subway fare was a nickel, stations were cleaned at night, and there was no more than a five-minute wait for the "C" train. When fares got boosted to a dime, early fifties, everyone screamed but paid up.

I'm against revisionist history, too. Let Ivy League professors pursue that bent in 700-page books with 100 pages of footnotes. In the performing arts, revisionists have loudly taken over. You dare not give viewing time to Al Jolson in blackface. *My Fair Lady* now ends with Eliza slamming the door behind her, rejecting Professor Higgins, who treated her as a servant. Let Higgins get his own slippers.

There are reservations about showing *Gone with the Wind* now. Even *The Most Happy Fella*, which I'd like to revive, needs lots of touching up. Women can no longer be put in a meat-market situation. Tony, that male chauvinist, dared to trick Rosabella with a young man's photograph. What's to do? Change Shakespeare's Shylock into a waspy banker in grey flannels? Do we sanitize Othello into a more felicitous husband, not the jealous brute who snuffs his adoring wife?

The ultimate grandiosity is the Big Board selling near 20 times normalized earnings. Market historians like me would pontificate "not for long without an earnings story." Half my capital resides in junk bonds yielding 5.5%, the reciprocal of grandiosity. Even AT&T can be a big winner in a low-interest-rate setting, yielding over 6.5%. Analysts stick lukewarm to neutral. AT&T is no longer a long-lines telephone story but an entertainment conglomerate that's tough to construe in a definitive-earnings construct.

Now is not the time to live dangerously, grandly. Before 9/11, my old, old friend Sam Zell warned me never to live or work in a landmark building. Too dangerous. The grave dancer knew what he was talking about. John Lennon was gunned down by a nebbish, a wannabe, at the entrance of the Dakota, coming home from a studio rehearsal in Times Square. Big-city newspapers, once great franchises before the internet, now are owned as hobby horses by operators like Jeff Bezos. Even Sam bought a Chicago chain. Nobody's exempt.

Corporate grandiosity no longer gets expressed in fleets of jet aircraft, the erection of the General Motors building and flashy art collections. We're down to hard-bone executive compensation: huge stock grants, outsized bonus allotments and stock options. Tesla and Boeing are my prime examples of excess, but in previous cycles, such largesse took place in the energy sector as well as technology and the Street's financial houses.

Grandiosity in stocks on the Big Board covers ponies tracking over $1,000

Flee Grandiosity, the Killer White Whale

a share. We're talking Amazon, Alphabet, Berkshire Hathaway and Tesla. In the old days, everyone split their stock down to $50 to attract new buyers. A $1,000 stock now is the ultimate finger gesture. "Sorry, fellas. We don't need you any longer." Subconsciously, this has led me to focus more on my ragamuffins.

There are ironies herein. Amazon and Tesla don't submit themselves to conventional security analysis. Everyone's shooting in the dark. I've added to Alibaba and Microsoft, which are analyzable. My moon shots remain—Halliburton and Freeport-McMoRan, washed out months ago under $5, now ticking over $10. They'll see $20 sooner or later.

My Dive-Bombing White Swans

What's in store for investors in our post-COVID-19 world? For sure, investment-grade debt is overpriced and under-yielding. The country's deficit sticks close to 100% of GDP for the decade. Largesse is over for the corporate tax rate, while givebacks from the wealthy rest in the cards.

Life sticks unfair for the middle class, particularly young adults. There's a screaming need for free college tuition, but where's the money for it? States and municipalities are in over their heads with balance-sheet debt and fiscal deficits. At least, home mortgage rates at 3% are a bargain, historically speaking, and could stick there for years.

Stress and pressure. It reminds me of my white swan pair who turned into vicious lake fighters, rejecting an invading black swan couple. Biting, hissing and flapping their wings hysterically, they drove off the intruders. My lake façade of bucolic serenity was as treacherous as the stock market churning near new-high ground at midyear 2020.

On my place in the Hudson Valley, red-winged blackbirds and robins returned a week too early and met a 10-inch snowfall. Nobody's timing is perfect. Maybe our market has discounted already the coming cyclical recovery. But I do believe tech paper holds its own. Nobody takes away my Microsoft, Facebook, Alibaba and Amazon.

Forge your own working model for the next couple of years. Don't trust any economist unless he shows you his past three years' tax returns. I'm at a max-capitalization rate of 15 times earnings. Let's hope I'm too conservative,

My Dive-Bombing White Swans

that the market has room.

First, some market history:

In the seventies and eighties, the market contended with Dr. Doom (Henry Kaufman) as well as Dr. Death (Al Wojnilower). Henry was a senior partner at Salomon Brothers, and Al was house economist at First Boston. Henry perennially feared irrepressible inflation and sky-high interest rates. Al usually found our economic system on the verge of dysfunctionality, but never opined, wisely, on the stock market's course. Neither did Henry, an old and wise friend.

Bond traders at Solly and First Boston routinely ignored their resident gurus, but both economists were widely respected, fearlessly standing alone, outside their brethren's consensus. Kaufman published annually Solly's widely read report on the supply and demand for funds in the U.S. This was bedrock research for projecting interest rates over the next 12 months. Everyone read it.

Pre–Black Monday, late 1987, the market sold at 20 times earnings. LBO money cost 8% then, with preferred stock for deals costing 12% or more. Debt coverage was skimpy. American Airlines raising capital by offering a convertible debenture with a 6% coupon reminds me of all this past nonsense. The Treasury Department then considered disallowing interest expense on deals, but was talked out of their position by Wall Street's honchos. Thank the Lord!

Corporate finance departments dictated to analysts what they should write about on specific deals. A mild recession in 2001 followed the blowup herein.

After 9/11, the housing boom took over and mortgage-credit excesses nearly destroyed our financial system, starting with our biggest banks, like Citigroup, and then Merrill Lynch's demise. But the U.S. Treasury and FRB stepped in to save the Street from its insane mufti-pufti. Rarely remarked upon, even to this day, is valuation was overstretched in 2007, pre the meltdown. Like today, the market sold at 20 times perceived normalized earnings. Hard to be a winner.

It reminded me of when I used to play tic-tac-toe against the glass-caged chicken in Chinatown. The bird always got first move so I couldn't possibly win. She got to eat seeds while I was out a quarter. One helluva agile chicken!

There's a limit to federal assistance for college tuition. The country should require at least a year of public service in return for financing four years of college. State and municipal pension funds won't meet actuarial assumptions. God only knows how such liabilities are met.

If corporate and individual tax rates show an upward Biden slope, it's unlikely to be steep. The rate of return on equity for major corporations should remain intact, on the high side. I'm more impressed with management initiatives this cycle than 50 years ago. Our trillion-dollar corporations like Amazon, Microsoft and Apple are better managed than Xerox, Polaroid and IBM were.

Pre-COVID-19, the country was benefiting from a more normalized setting where interest rates, disposable income and consumption were expressed in rising earnings, escalating price-earnings ratios and manageable inflation. The COVID-19 monkey wrench overcame summary forecasts made at yearend 2019.

Deflation, mid-2020, pervaded the setting in the country. Unemployment rolls reached Great Depression percentages. Deflationary pricing existed throughout the commodities sector, starting with oil and going down to steel, copper and aluminum. My feel is the industrial sector makes its comeback in 2021, but these stocks are fully priced and don't deserve to sell at 18 to 20 times earnings. Starting with AT&T, higher dividend-paying capacity is minimal. Such companies as Exxon Mobil, DuPont, Caterpillar, etc. show little or no growth in free cash flow, unlikely to change much next couple of years. Deflation sticks around.

The stock market, based on earnings recovery and dividend-paying capacity, is fully priced-in, even with protracted minimal interest rates. The emotional content of the market is remarkable in day-to-day volatility, how rapidly optimism turns into pessimism and then back. A week later, everyone's ready to discount economic recovery around the corner. The oil surplus, worldwide, gets sopped up, right?

Not so fast. The U.S. is now an exporter of oil, no longer running a deficit over one million barrels. The Saudis' public sale of its tranche of Aramco got done, but everyone shoulda turned their backs on such a pricey offering. Shut-in capacity is long standing for steel, aluminum, even copper, next couple of years. Without some commodity inflation, the market is a stillborn thing.

My Dive-Bombing White Swans

I'm sold on technology next couple of years. Trillion-dollar capitalizations like Apple, Amazon and Microsoft hold share of market in cellular telephony, cloud computing and e-commerce coverage. They are huge free-cash-flow machines that spend enormous sums on R&D.

Today, the half-dozen properties comprising over 20% of the market's capitalization are at least 150% as volatile as the S&P 500 Index. If I'm wrong and these properties soon peak out, the market is in for a serious whipping. Technology already dominates sector weighting for the index, maybe headed for 30%, an unprecedented, scary dominance, but explainable.

The passive investor should use balanced index funds with ETFs for high-yield bonds. Hold 10% to 20% in the NASDAQ-100 Index to capture meaningful internet and e-commerce weighting. As for ragamuffins, you need some diversification, not just one or two, but half a dozen. You pick 'em, but under 10 bucks. Mine are Halliburton, Freeport-McMoRan, and Energy Transfer.

Finally, don't allow the market to torture you. Sell down to your sleeping level whenever you feel like doing so. Take yourself off leverage. I do leverage myself in junk bonds because borrowing costs are minimal. Deep down, all assets are impacted by the cost-of-carry, now a big plus for junk.

Our federal government needs lots of income to reduce its outsized deficit relative to GDP. Hard for me to see corporate tax rates not trending higher by five percentage points. The largesse is over for individual taxpayers with capital gains tax rates destined higher.

Fearfully, I thumbed through my historical charts on market valuation relative to interest rates and capitalized earnings. For how many years might market returns remain next to nothing? My trendline for price-earnings ratios goes back to 1985 when the market sold at 10 times earnings, but reached 15 times pre–Black Monday (1987). Take out the insane level of 25 reached during the tech bubble of 2000–'01. Before the financial meltdown, 2007, we sat at 15 times earnings, too. It was easy to draw the appropriate trendline covering over three decades. It was 15 times earnings, which is what I'm comfortable with today.

Trump, The Murphy Man

My father was a frugal operator by necessity, not choice. Pop settled for his bowl of kasha, wolfing it down like the Russian peasant he was.

If I were such a success, where was my yacht and string of racehorses? *They* wouldn't let his son make serious money. The *Theys* knew everything, and his son couldn't be in with the *Theys*.

Pop was wrong. There is no *They*. Theoretically, Freudians skilled in dream analysis should make great investors, stripping off the tinsel and fathoming the essence of a corporation's psyche and the sentiment that surrounds the company, its image and the preconceptions of the Street, as to what the facts portend. In practice, few can isolate pivotal variables—reality.

The stock market packages petty and vicarious dreams, each stock symbol another story. If you're a natural, you can envision tomorrow's stock tables. Don't ask me how it's done. You're either a moneymaker or just another quant in the system. There are a couple of dozen operators in the country with capacity to think so abstractly that they know what today's economic and political pressures mean for tomorrow's financial markets, worldwide. Nobody gets it all right, but you can come close.

In the sixties, the Dow Jones news ticker would ring a bell every time there was some good news. It was the custom for some junior analyst to race to the ticker and yell out the story to the research department. "IBM splits three for one," whatever. One day, I heard the ticker sounding off every half hour like in a firehouse. It was Joe Granville, our market letter writer, now hustling over, first

Trump, The Murphy Man

to devour the news. "General Motors declares regular dividend," the teleprinter jiggled out. "My God!" Joe exclaimed. "They're ringing the bell for nothing new," Joe whispered to me. "It's all over." He was right on the money.

Mid-2020, I was feeling like Joe. I expected Dow Jones to ring bells that banks were opening for business, regularly, at 9:00 a.m. There were times when I felt like a number, particularly when I contested for control of Caesars World in the eighties. It was Mike Milken on the phone:

"You don't understand, Marty. Management sees you all the same way. There's no difference between you and Carl Icahn. No management is going to stand by and let you gobble up their stock. One day it's 15%, then it's 25%, and then you want it all. You're like Hitler to them."

"I'm not Hitler and I don't have enough money to buy it all."

"Why should they assume you're not Hitler?"

"Mike, we'll have another conversation."

"It's heading in the wrong direction," Mike said. "The lawyers smell fee money."

I heard some junk bond quotes in the background and hung up.

I had grown up in the East Bronx during the Great Depression. Our family of five lived in three rooms, a walk-up, on the third floor, the rent $40 a month. Don't ask me why, but all apartments were painted in baby blue and pink. What landlords ordered from their painting crews. How to get out of the Bronx, away from pink and blue walls and the 9' x 12' bedrooms? Standard 3/4" gypsum wallboard boxed in the space. Cheap, hollow-wooded veneer doors slammed shut from the slightest of drafts. "Getting out" was the rallying call that led to Nobel Prize winners, Pulitzer Prizes, billionaires, everything except maybe four-star generals and the presidency—so far.

Thirty-five years after getting out, I was living in approximately the same square footage, but at a better address than 964 Sherman Avenue. The Trump Tower zips up from 57th Street and Fifth Avenue, an elongated glissando of glitz some 65 stories high. For $1 million you got 1,200 square feet there, probably the most expensive residential square footage in the world. The Beverly

153

Train to Outslug the Market

Hills crowd made their pads here. Seasoned Gucci-wise Asians, Latinos and Arabs bought these apartments because the boards of cooperative buildings preferred less peripatetic owners. We called it "the closet in the sky," and it was just about big enough to store all of my wife's clothes. For a while we considered making it one giant cedar closet, but the implicit cost—over $10,000 a month in interest lost on our $1 million—made the hurdle rate a bit steep.

The view from the 59th floor was instructive. You saw practically nothing but the tops of other buildings, hardly any Hudson River and just a tip of New York Harbor. New York is a real-estate-dominated town, and the pols rarely get in the way of big-time developers who would parcel out Central Park among themselves if given the chance and bid on the air rights over the Hudson River.

We were one of the first owners to move into our closet in the sky, and just so you know that the idle rich have their problems, too, let me tell you what it was like living practically alone in the Trump Tower. The air conditioner was a sometime thing, the toilet flushometers performed like asthmatics, and the hot water took 40 minutes to reach our level.

There was no intercom hooked up with the front desk. The elevator service required a phone call to the concierge to get us. God help us if the phone lines were tied up! It was time for me to have a little talk with Donald Trump, so I wrote him about my cold-water flat in the sky and asked him to call me.

"Marty! I'm so sorry you had to write a letter like that. Marty, we are putting your apartment on Red Alert. Whatever we can do to make you happy, Marty."

"Donald, I wake up in the morning and I can't use the facilities. I can't take a hot bath unless I get up at six a.m. and then the air-conditioning cuts off, and the elevator is hit and miss. Donald, your building doesn't work."

"Marty, I wish you wouldn't say that. We have a fabulous building. And the lobby, Marty, isn't it fantastic! The marble and view from your apartment, Marty? The Best!"

"Donald, I look out at the tops of buildings. I am eye-to-eye with huge neon signs that say RCA and 666 and Newsweek and the time in 22-foot numerals."

"Marty, how many people can look out their windows and see the tops of

Trump, The Murphy Man

such fantastic buildings?"

"Donald, the air-conditioning is too sophisticated. It cuts off because not enough people are living in the building."

"Marty, we are going to simulate a fully inhabited building so you can have your air-conditioning."

"Donald, I thank you. But what do I do for an elevator? You are always checking them out, so they never run. My wife used the construction elevator and I haven't seen her for three days. She is being passed around among two hundred construction workers, Donald. The last I heard, they made her into a runner peddling football pools between the 30th and 65th floors.

"Donald, forty minutes for hot water. Can you simulate full occupancy so the computer will be nice to me?"

"Marty, I already told you we have put you on Red Alert. And don't forget the party in the atrium."

The promoter's blitz was over and I stared out at old 666. A police siren pierced the 59th-story aloofness. That was Tishman's place—by now, probably fully depreciated by three consecutive owners at higher resale values with little or no paid taxes to the city, state and federal governments. In fact, the tax laws encourage accelerated depreciation on commercial real estate that never seems to depreciate at all.

But my standard of living had depreciated greatly since the old Bronx days. I missed the smell of baked potatoes on every stair landing in the old walk-up. From a working microwave oven there is only the electronic, odorless beep… beep…beep.

We sold out after a year and moved to a place where hot water and elevator service were timely.

22

Obtain, Maintain, Then Compound Wealth

First, a brief history of markets:
- Thirty-year Treasuries currently yield 1.5%, but in 1982 during FRB tightening hit 15%. Five-year paper, a comparable trajectory.
- Dollar depreciation or appreciation can range between minus 25% and plus 25%.
- Deep-seated financial risk lurks in almost every type of asset. Banks capitalized at $200 billion can self-destruct with hidden bad loans. American International Group needed a government package of $180 billion to remain solvent after guaranteeing sub-prime loans.
- Municipalities, even countries, can bankrupt themselves. Consider Greece and Venezuela. Brazil, Iceland and Thailand were world-destabilizing forces through their over-leveraged banks, even though their GDPs were minuscule. Chicago, Detroit, Sacramento, possibly New Jersey currently and New York City some 20 years ago saw the wolf at the door.
- Puerto Rico now hovers near basket-case status.
- You need a specialist manager for high-yield securities. They'd need to log a risk-adjusted return way above investment-grade bonds. A high-yield bond ETF is suitable as a passive investment.

Remember, NASDAQ-100 is volatile. But 10% of assets here is OK. This index appreciated 45% last year. Don't get involved in whether growth stocks or value paper is preferable. In the long run, both come out neck 'n' neck. Avoid emerging-market equities and small-capitalization stocks, which seem best left to intensive stock market operators.

Investing offshore is laden with serious variables. Not just geopolitical risk but sizable currency exposure. Foreign accounting standards remain far less rigorous than ours. Stay away from managers who spread client capital over 20 or more investment categories, a themeless pie-chart construct that usually underperforms.

How to Focus Yourself:

- **Don't invest in properties where you've concluded management is not socially responsible or its headman's character is impeachable.**
- **As Warren Buffett has written, you don't want to bet against America going back to George Washington's presidency. No short selling or naked options writing necessary. You'll screw up your head and at best break even.**
- **Never wax emotional about what you own nor live in the past. Consider icons like IBM, General Electric, Polaroid, Eastman Kodak and Xerox are either gone, diminished or discredited.**
- **Remember you're just a number on a broker's ledger. Give them no discretion over your account and don't listen to their recommendations.**

Consider, the average life of a growth stock hardly lasts over five years, and only 5% hang in for a decade or more. Your image of a corporation's viability and competitive mettle is probably five to 10 years out-of-date. They don't know you own their stock or that you love it passionately because of their latest-model car.

Never forget the Street's optimism repeatedly transfers itself into pessimism, sometimes practically overnight. The forces that created the bull market

Train to Outslug the Market

and bonds are unlikely to change much in coming years. I'm talking about low commodity prices, moderate wage inflation and more punitive individual and corporate taxation that get legislated. Although the slowdown in economic growth may not be fully discounted, it seems manageable in a low interest-rate environment.

Avoid mature companies in manufacturing or materials and mining starting with coal, steel and aluminum. No flow of dividends there can result in a good return to investors considering price-earnings ratios here remain in teens.

We are in the midst of a major-positive technological upswing nowhere near maturity re: internet, e-commerce, cloud computing and personal computer services.

The proposed investment construct depending on the need for annualized income:

> • **Maintain 50% or less of investment capital in an index fund such as Vanguard or Fidelity. Fees are minimal along with ease of entry and exit.**
>
> • **For income, keep 50% or more of assets in a high-yield bond fund with a yield approximating 5%. Investment quality should average BB with duration of five years. Invesco manages such a fund, appropriately diversified.**
>
> • **Avoid investment counselors at banks and brokerage houses, hedge fund operators, et al. Performance records do run below benchmark goals while fees are at least 1% plus profit participation. Avoid 2% portfolio fee constructs. Long term, fees detract meaningfully from results. Particularly avoid wealth-management houses that employ pie-chart schemata that invest in everything—gold, oil futures, offshore debt and equity, etc. They are long-term underperformers.**
>
> • **The reason for NASDAQ-100 exposure is the country remains in a technological upswing nowhere near maturity— internet, e-commerce and cloud computing. Think of RCA's color TV, Polaroid and Xerox 60 years ago. But remember:**

The average life of a growth stock is five years, some at 10 years. Don't get much involved in stock picking.

- **PORTFOLIO STRUCTURE MUST BE YOUR PRIMARY FOCUS.**

You can't show money-management prowess working at it sporadically. If you want to manage your own capital with intensity, allocate 50 hours, weekly, get yourself an MBA and lease a Bloomberg console. Cream puffs only wax rich accidentally.

Deviate from these precepts, and like the *Commendatore* in *Don Giovanni*, I'll come back in a shroud and intone dolorously, *"Repent!... Repent!"* The Don, remember, came to a sorry demise, engulfed in flames and dragged off to hell like an inside trader.

* For income, keep 50% of assets in a high-yield bond fund when yield approximates 5%. Investment quality should be BB minimal, with duration of portfolio averaging out at five years.

* For exposure to growth stocks, at least 10% of your portfolio should be in an ETF that captures the NASDAQ-100 Index. This is a volatile construct but gives good exposure to Microsoft, Apple, Facebook, Alphabet, et al. Where yield and volatility are not of primary concern, exposure to NASDAQ-100 can be increased to 25% while lowering the percentage invested in an S&P Index fund.

23

Hope I'm Too Pessimistic

When can we see normalized growth for our country? Trick question. You never see normalized annual GDP growth of 3%. It's always more or less than 3%. Economists, actually nobody, ever gets it right. Mid-2020, the market was busily discounting a huge economic recovery in store for the country. Maybe yes, maybe no.

Viciously cyclical properties like oil service plays, Halliburton and Schlumberger, popped 100% and 50%, spring 2020. Even General Electric, Ford Motor, U.S. Steel and Alcoa showed some late foot. Not that growth stocks like Amazon, Facebook and Microsoft turned into wallflowers. Facebook rallied 50% off its March 2020 low. Bad publicity couldn't quash it.

In securities markets, life is unfair. I remember my father calling General Motors "a son of a bitch" along with Royal Dutch Petroleum and U.S. Steel. These were the odd lots their "customer's man" put them into late forties, early fifties. Blue Chips fluctuated plenty then, but never made my parents rich. It was called "Owning a slice of America." If you liked the new Ford '52-model compact station wagon for $1,900, you bought a round lot of Ford, too. Portable electric typewriters were an innovation then, so buy Smith Corona. Life was simplistic. I found my mother's mildewed stock certificates in her steamer trunk.

Seventy years later, we're dealing with $1.5 trillion market capitalizations like Amazon, which still showed a skimpy bottom line. Facebook sold at six times book value. Jeff Bezos, Bill Gates and Mark Zuckerberg benefited from the heady capitalized valuation of their control positions, not earnings and

Hope I'm Too Pessimistic

dividends, which twinkle on the horizon.

Passive investors need to face the facts of bewildering quarterly reports short on interpretation. This won't change. Conceptually, you want to own stocks good for the next five years, but not even Warren Buffett got it right, owning value paper when technology came on strong.

Normally, a $1,000 stock radiates more motive force than a $5 piece of paper. It gets more press coverage and frequent iPad updates. There's no valley to look over. E-commerce and internet houses remain unchecked growth stories. You do need to understand how analysts capitalize their numbers. If Amazon's revenues are up 21%, but the Street expected 29%, the stock tanks overnight and vice-versa.

The best an armchair investor can do is make a judgment call on the business cycle—interest rates and inflation as they apply to his inventory of stocks. Is GDP likely to accelerate or diminish? What is the Federal Reserve Board likely to do next 12 months, and what about the course of energy prices and other materials like copper, steel and aluminum? Is speculation going to permeate the air or bearishness? Nobody is perfect, but you can monitor trend and direction, then adjust your inventory. **Conceptually, you want to own stocks good for the next five years, not ponder whether General Motors cuts its dividend tomorrow.**

There are entire industries leveraged with debt that individuals shouldn't ever play. Include airlines, autos, most of retailing, oil and gas production excepting MLPs with adequate yield coverage. Many industrials and materials producers look fully priced with no stories attached to them. Same goes for banks unless you're wildly bullish on GDP momentum and elevated interest rates.

Nearly weekly, at times daily, waves of pessimism overcome currents of market optimism. Nobody can claim the inside track on timing the COVID-19 vaccine breakthrough. At midyear, I assumed the vaccine was a year away, but the back-to-work movement could forge ahead. The Fed doggedly holds money market rates near zero. So, get busy discounting the successful transition to a normalized economy with above-average GDP momentum lasting for a couple of years. If you don't buy this scenario, the market belongs at 2,500, not 3,100.

I'm passionate in belief the country preserves its technological growth condition:

e-commerce, cloud computing, internet connectivity and cellular telephony. The entertainment industry manages its comeback, too. Stay cautious on basic industrials, oil and the commodity sector. Overcapacity prevails in oil, copper, steel and aluminum. Basic-industrial earnings power reasserts itself, slowly, but present price-earnings ratios already discount much of the recovery.

My Overweighted Sectors and Stocks:

Cloud computing – Microsoft, Amazon, Alibaba

E-commerce – Amazon, Alibaba

Internet providers – Facebook, Alphabet

Cellular telephony – T-Mobile

Oil services – Halliburton

Entertainment – Walt Disney

High-yield bonds – Invesco ETF

Commodities – Freeport-McMoRan

MLPs – Enterprise Products Partners, Williams Partners

Is the world's shoe on the wrong foot, deflation not inflation? Such a malaise could last a couple of years. There's surplus oil and gas capacity. Same goes for steel, copper and aluminum. New commercial construction—office space, hotels and 50-story condominiums for the top 0.1%—could need years of absorption. Shopping centers may not sign up new core AAA tenants like the old Macy's and Sears, Roebuck, now struggling. Replacement by shaky fitness centers with low credit ratings won't do the job.

It's hard to anticipate much pent-up demand in key industrial sectors like automobiles. There's too much capacity, and worldwide revenue is stalled out in Europe and the Far East. The aerospace sector can take years to be rationalized. Excess capacity besets airlines. Who knows how fast air traffic, both business and personal, regains its footing?

Hope I'm Too Pessimistic

I never expected to see capital markets wobble with such minimal interest rates in Treasuries, AAA corporates and a near-zero money market. For much of our postwar financial history, high interest rates and inflation were depressive factors. The proactive Federal Reserve Board took interest rates up to 15% in 1982, and on the eve of Black Monday loan rates were pressing to 8%. The Fed now fears zero-to-negative rates would depress the country. This is the nonsense of economists.

Low interest rates hold single-family mortgage rates at 3.25%, a powerful stimulant for home ownership. Corporations with low credit ratings, say BB, even single B, now find capital markets open. Look at American Airlines, raising billions. The press for yield by individual investors and pension funds is irrepressible and long lasting.

Near-zero rates can be regenerative for the stock market. Mid-2020, the market blithely ignored any lasting impact from COVID-19. This surprised me, that stocks early on got busy discounting earnings recovery. Nobody paid any attention to the costs of carrying the unemployed along with shut-in industries like airlines and retailing.

Maybe this is a $10 trillion bill that gets added onto our existing deficit. The ratio of debt to GDP is going above 100%, a banana-republic kind of number. Nobody cares, but I wouldn't buy tax-exempt bonds, ever. Hopefully, Washington doesn't tell New York City to drop dead again, like the Daily News headlined 45 years ago.

If I had to average my cost of capital, I'd put it at 6% over 60 years. Interest rates under 1% have turned me into an active arbitrageur of capital. I've built up a huge portfolio of high-yield bonds. Fear of recession keeps spreads between BB bonds, AAAs and Treasuries very attractive for junk. New York City, remember, sold bonds yielding 8% back in the early seventies. Residual buyers were the municipal unions and they came out whole. I wasn't smart enough to buy this paper. New York City was in a deep real-estate funk during 1973–'74. Today, maintaining 40% of your assets in high-quality fixed income paper like Treasuries and AAA corporates is a loser's game. But I project my BB bonds'

Train to Outslug the Market

total return next 12 months at 10%.

Some 60 years ago, I soared on Boeing's 707 jet introduction. Zenith and RCA gave us color television. The transistor's invention opened up technology plays like Texas Instruments, Motorola and Fairchild Camera. IBM bet the farm developing its 360 computer and won. Remington Rand and Burroughs pooped out. I knew about successful development of Syntex's "pill" before approval by the FDA and played it with options galore.

The reason Warren Buffett was so successful early on with stocks like American Express was that Wall Street research was as yet primitive, even early sixties. Too many statisticians left over from 1929 just thumbed through dusty financial manuals like Moody's and Standard and Poor's.

The advent of technology, early sixties, created a new class of adventuresome analysts who enacted serious fieldwork and talked to everybody contending for industry hegemony, like Texas Instruments. I believed Fairchild Camera walked on water, and they did for years. My Syntex never renewed itself with great R&D productivity. Birth control pills proliferated from several other drug houses.

I'll never change my game—growth stocks and a sprinkling of ragamuffins to quicken blood circulation. Vanity pushes me into pretending I can handle change at the margin, which is what this game boils down to, like it or not.

I'll never allow vanity to compel me to pretend I can plan every step worth taking, but you do need a working hypothesis. My working number is a price-earnings ratio around 15. The yield on Treasuries works its way back up to between 3% and 4%. Inflation doesn't surface as a regulatory issue for several years. The S&P 500 Index at 3,100 stands nearly 20% overvalued. It could take the recovering economy three years to catch up with lagging overvaluation.

With taxes likely to rise across the board, corporate and individual, we're headed into a difficult cycle for capital formation. Gold bugs won't get any richer, either, if we solve COVID-19. Late in 1980, oil looked golden, too, but got destroyed over 12 months.

The problem with our COVID-19 torture is that the market already has re-

Hope I'm Too Pessimistic

covered from its spring of 2020 malaise and sells at 20 times earnings. All other historical depressants mentioned here put the market down to 10 times earnings, yielding 5% and selling at book value. Nobody promised us a rose garden.

What shapes a great stock market cycle is solid economic growth—3% to 4% per annum. I'm not sure it's coming. I bank on continued momentum for the technology sector. But, for armchair players, capital formation seems iffy. Bonds are overpriced, enormously, and could decline for years.

All these provisos shape my heavy cross to shoulder. Let's hope I'm crazy pessimistic. And yet, coming soon, the tax rate for corporations wends higher. I see a steeper take on capital gains while plutocrats get slapped, annually, on their outstanding fortunes. I've assumed President Trump should be toast.

Buoyant equity cycles normally follow from depressed valuation as experienced in 1973–'74, the Cuban Missile Crisis, Paul Volcker's dosage of 15% interest rates and post the tech bubble of 2000 and the financial meltdown of 2008–'09. Off its March 2020 low, the market traded into new high ground by July. Too much, too soon?

This chart on 10-year Treasury bond yields is a sobering picture. I didn't expect to see interest rates so high for so long. I'd draw a trendline through 5%, not today's 60 basis points. X-out the early eighties peak of 15%. It was induced by the FRB to stamp out the rampant inflationary bias in the economy. The financial market's meltdown of 2008–'09 crushed rates convincingly below 5%.

Deflation won't last forever. We'll look back on negative interest rates as a curiosity of institutional stupidity. The market needs three years of strong earnings to catch up with present valuation. Bonds now stand crazily overpriced, and probably soften for years. A bull market starting from mid-2020's elevated level seems far-fetched.

Digging deep down into my shoes, I felt our markets belonged to operators and traders, not long-cycle passive investors. Pie-chart diversification won't work, either. If you're afraid of NASDAQ -100 and BB debentures, don't be fully committed in an overpriced setting.

Train to Outslug the Market

10-YEAR TREASURY BOND HISTORY

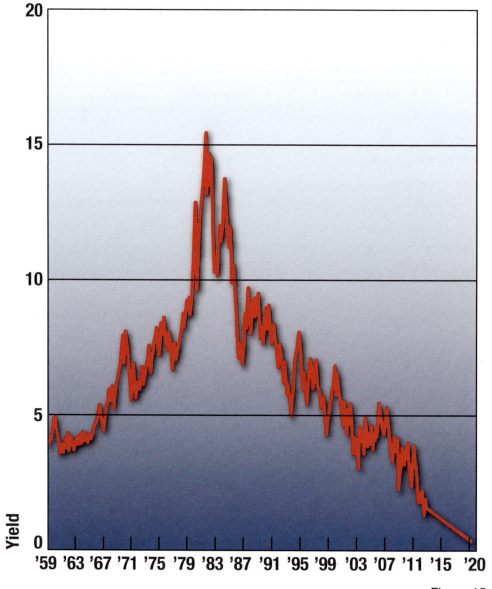

Figure 15
Source: Federal Reserve Board

CONCLUSION

FRB Wimp-out Bullish
for Growthies

I've struggled over 60 years to outfox the FRB. You do this by projecting what will be in their heads 12 months out, not by currently voiced concerns reported in the press.

The Fed is in a mode of absurd doublespeak and wish fulfillment. No inflation, currently, and this is bad for the economy. What's more, they won't raise interest rates even after inflation ratchets back to 2%. So…all you consumers out there, spend your savings, buy first homes and shop until you drop. Treat yourself to a new car while the cost of carry hangs so low.

With 30-year Treasuries yielding 1.49%, 10-year paper at 70 basis points and the two-year notes at 20 basis points, the Fed would be first to say the market has taken away historic powers to reset interest rates, influence the economic cycle, up or down, and combat inflation and the unemployment rate.

This was not always the case. My favorite FRB chairman is Andrew Mellon, who viewed most industrialists as dumb bunnies who created inventory and capital goods recessions by their periodic overspending. His was the right call that repeated itself into the sixties.

President Franklin Roosevelt despised Mellon for his harsh response to corporate sector exuberance. Always an astute banker, Mellon inventoried a conservative loan portfolio, believing recurrent business cycles were a given every five years. Roosevelt prompted the U.S. Treasury to sue him for tax evasion. Mellon died before the case was decided in his favor. His collection of Italian Renaissance art became the nucleus of the National Gallery of Art in our capital,

Train to Outslug the Market

endowed by Mellon, actually designed by his architects.

In our time, Federal Reserve Board Chairmen like Paul Volcker, McChesney Martin and Alan Greenspan stand out. Volcker practically bankrupted the country, pressing on 15% interest rates, but he bled out inflationary expectations then rising at a 7% to 8% clip.

Alan Greenspan proved the most energized chairman, super proactive. When Greenspan dropped the Federal Funds rate 50 basis points, January 2001, NASDAQ rallied overnight nearly 15%. We all got busy discounting coming economic expansion.

When Jerry Goodman (Adam Smith), my old, old buddy, now gone, was interviewing Greenspan, he asked Alan if what he did was fun. Greenspan probably never fielded such a question and he seemed nonplussed. Jerry had blindsided the oracle who said: "Well, not exactly."

Unfortunately, central bankers don't trash-talk like standup comics, who themselves can be filled with wisdom. Not just in the U.S., but in Japan, England and Germany, central banker verbiage is interchangeable, dull and most unlikely to catch oncoming inflection points.

I assume anyone who invests seeks an above-average return on capital, but maybe not always so. For some, playing the market is like playing the ponies, a mindless distraction. For my brother-in-law, all his capital rested in short-term paper. He doesn't care that T-bills carry a near-zero rate of return, but wants to sleep secure, his capital safe and available when called for. He's right in his own frame of reference.

I'm at the other end of the investment spectrum, craving the moon, but still research-based in my picks. Being fundamentally right and overweighted in Apple, Facebook, Alibaba, Amazon and Microsoft is a derivative of my belief that disinflation lasts for years and the FRB has no tools to deal with it.

The plight of our stagnating middle class can be laid at the feet of globalization of industrial manufacturing capacity, decades ago, the move to low-cost sources in the Far East, even South America. U.S. industry capacity utilization is likely to remain low, meaning employment rolls stick flattish in the U.S. for

FRB Wimp-out Bullish for Growthies

years ahead.

If domestic interest rates snake along ground zero, the price-earnings multiplier for growth stocks holds in new high ground. Curiously, the recent changes in the Dow Jones Industrials list put the emphasis on growth. The Dow Jones should drop "Industrials" from its name. It is no longer descriptive of this index, which more and more looks like the S&P 500 Index.

Wisely, to remain competitive as an index, the Dow can't count any longer on stocks like Exxon Mobil, halved by the market past five years. I regard pre-technology market leaders before 1960 as the uninvestables. Stocks like U.S. Steel, Alcoa, General Electric, even General Motors and Ford Motor sport overleveraged balance sheets and stagnant demand for their output.

I'm a player in materials stocks like Freeport-McMoRan because it got oversold. Same goes for Halliburton, which has tripled in a matter of three months, its high over $29, low under five bucks. I've bought a bunch of MLPs like Enterprise Products Partners and Williams, hoping their distributive cash flow holds up, that oil futures don't tank.

My most believed-in play on the persistence of minimal interest rates is the high-yield market for corporate debentures. Here, I'm arbitraging money, as well. My cost of carry doesn't exceed 1% on a portfolio of debentures with five-year duration, yielding over 5%. I'll be wrong only if the country sinks into deep depression or interest rates spike several hundred basis points. At least, I've got the Federal Reserve Board on my side.

Over sixty years, averaging my costs on borrowed capital, I come out somewhere between 6% and 7%. FRB chairman McChesney Martin was my nemesis in the sixties. When inflation reared its head, he'd take away the punchbowl, spiking margin requirements to 90% while money market rates shot up unmercifully. I turned to money brokers to fuel my obsession with convertible bonds like Boeing, United Aircraft and Eastern Air Lines, which all doubled and tripled as the jet age unfolded in the world.

The shoe's on the other foot now. Unless you believe an effective COVID-19 vaccine is around the corner (I don't), these stocks are the untouchables, bleed-

Train to Outslug the Market

ing capital, day after day.

In case you're wondering why I haven't mentioned our present FRB chairman by name, it's because it doesn't register on me as yet. He's faceless. Contrastingly, Alan Greenspan with his "Greenspeak" was embedded in our consciousness. Alan was great stepping in with a liquidity infusion day after Black Monday.

I've reservations on whether Alan read the nineties as well as the late eighties. He completely ignored ominous fiscal drag during the Clinton administration. Approximately 50 changes in the discount rate between Greenspan's ascendency to his post in 1987 and his retirement in 2006. If nothing else, all this plastered Alan on the front page, periodically. Nobody then caught the variable of the public reducing its savings rate to near zero.

By autumn of 2000, retail sales hit a stone wall. The market was in the throes of its tech bubble, which then crushed the NASDAQ 100 and put the country into recession. By mid-2000 I sensed that unconsciously, the adulation of Washington had gotten to Greenspan. Too many small changes in Fed Funds, sometimes bimonthly. Nobody wanted to deal with the need of a huge upfront tax cut.

Consider, after Paul Volcker crushed inflationary expectations in 1982, it made Greenspan's job a snap. In the summer of 1982, the S&P 500 touched down at 100 (yes, 100) and peaked at 1,400 some 18 years later.

Greenspan once opined that you never recognize bubbles until after the fact. Our investment problem, COVID-19 induced, is the reciprocal: When to anticipate a resurging setting. My answer: Not so fast. Let Jerome Powell sleep through all this because whatever he says has no meaning for financial markets. His pronouncement that he wouldn't raise interest rates even if inflation reached 2% adumbrates the powerless FRB, no new tools at hand.

Actually, Powell took a page out of Ben Bernanke's book. Ben kept telling everyone who'd listen that low interest rates would rest in place for the foreseeable future, at least two years. Janet Yellen also talked this talk. Late in 2013, stock pros finally believed Bernanke meant what he said. Risk then pervaded the air.

The country changed for the better after Paul Volcker's *lavage rapide*. Labor's givebacks started. Jimmy Hoffa's ghost could no longer threaten paralysis for the country's interstate commerce. Membership in the UAW peaked, and then General Motors closed down their second-floor cafeteria in the General Motors building on Fifth Avenue, a profligate utilization of high-priced square footage.

Jack Welch was the first corporate honcho to employ General Electric's prime credit rating to leverage its balance sheet and move into the financial services sector. By year end 2014 the Dow breached 18,000 after basing at 6,649 in 2009. General Electric in 2001 was number one in the S&P 500 Index, capitalized at $417 billion. Exxon Mobil was number three, right after Microsoft. But, by 2014, General Electric had dropped down the list, supplanted by Apple. The market was beginning to have second thoughts on GE's viability.

Exxon Mobil peaked out then, too, and technology began its five-year run (see table on page 000). My sense is that in an environment of the FRB favoring low interest rates, no questions asked—own growth stocks. Expansive price-earnings ratios usually reach 20, what we had during 2020 despite COVID-19's impact.

Don't ever expect our administration to do the right thing. In 2008, several FRB members remained anti-stimulus dissenters. The U.S. Treasury bailed out Bear Stearns but pushed Lehman Brothers into bankruptcy. European central bankers today are just as spineless, watching interest rates press into negative territory but resisting much fiscal stimulus. Our FRB came close to freezing up in the financial wreckage of 2009.

Never forget, rising bond yields top out any bull market within a year or two. The reciprocal is true, too. During the nineties, the 10-year yield on Treasuries started at 7.8%, then declined to 6% until 2000. The S&P 500 Index started out at 15 times earnings, but ended the decade near 30 times. Tracking the rate for Federal Funds, I was surprised to see it as low as 25 basis points in 2015 vs. its long-term trend at 4%. Nobody sees 4% coming back. Even a rise

Train to Outslug the Market

to 2% shouldn't panic the bond market. With 30-year Treasuries at 1.5%, even a rise to 3% shouldn't impact price-earnings ratios, considering a 4.5% yield is the long-term norm.

The Fed did panic in early 1984 when the economy, post Volcker's schmeiss, was booming. They put Treasuries up to a 13.5% yield and interest rates didn't break below 10% until late in 1985. At Black Monday in October they remained high, over 7%, then surged to 9.5% by summer of 1988. I remember deal money was tight. I was paying 8% for a standby credit line of $1 billion from a consortium of banks.

Then, prevailing conclusions in the country changed markedly. The FRB went from easing to tightening. Interest rates rose from 8½% to 9½%. Their fear of an overheating economy supplanted thinking on recession around the corner. Both conclusions proved erroneous. Post Paul Volcker's strong medicine, succeeding FRB chairmen like Janet Yellen prayed out loud for 2% inflation.

Economists term the assumption that nothing changes as the naïve forecast. That's what we had from the FRB throughout 2014 and it's what we're having now. Nobody's jittery about overstaying the easy-money construct. Stock market operators like me so far can live with extended valuations for e-commerce and tech houses like Amazon, Alibaba, Facebook, Microsoft and Apple. Let somebody else own General Motors and Exxon Mobil for a comeback.

I thought of all this as I watched my home-based white swan pair molt into vicious fighters. On my pond, they drove off an intruding swan couple—fighting, wings flapping, hissing, hysterically. Bucolic serenity is a myth best left to impressionist painters like Monet, I mused. My aquatic pets seemed a great metaphor for the Big Board, waxing ugly, then serene, then ugly once more.

Starting in 1988, the market saw fewer black swans paddling around. Yes, the Russians almost defaulted on their Treasury bills and the Fed zigged sometimes when it shoulda zagged. Later, the market in 2000 had to unsort the internet fiasco when stocks were rated on clicks. This was the Street's shabbiest interlude of pure decadence and ciphering stupidity.

The market is the great humbler. Everyone missed the call on the 1982 worldwide recession. It was the product of the Group of Seven's powerful monetarists led by Paul Volcker. Central bankers indulged in a séance of mutual emulation as to who could raise interest rates fastest and mostest.

We underestimated the staying power of central banks. Pre-Black Monday in late 1987, when Treasury Secretary Baker started to argue publicly with his counterpart in West Germany over relaxing the reins, financial markets overreacted, fearing contradictory policy initiatives. Deeply embedded in my head is the precept that the Fed always wins. It has more money and power at hand than you and me.

Riffling through 50 years of postwar-market stats is a humbling experience. Nobody is right on the money for very long. Too many upsets like wars, recessions, Federal Reserve Board insanity, galloping inflation and financial meltdowns like 2008 – 2009. Lay that one at the feet of our major banks and Wall Street houses.

A long time ago, I learned (painfully) never ride down a stock into single digits or even worse. You're supposed to buy stocks in single digits like Halliburton and Freeport-McMoRan just months ago. Halliburton has tripled off its low while Tesla is 30% off summer highs. Microsoft has eased along with Apple. Both sell around 30 times earnings power, so valuation has turned into a fundamental issue going forward.

Lemme tackle valuation structure before dealing with specific market sectors like technology and financials, together over 35% of S&P 500 Index weighting. Can anyone who's a serious player, say 60% or more of his capital in equity markets, make the case for staying the course? Further, can it remain a growth-stock play space or shift to the value sector, to industrials and energy where assets are bedrock, not clicks and headcount of active internet users?

For me, bedrock value derives from Tobin's Q Ratio. At a graduation ceremony at Bard College years ago, I had the pleasure of introducing James Tobin, the economist who birthed his Q Ratio. I was telling him how much I admired the elegance and simplicity of his insight.

Train to Outslug the Market

Briefly, the Q Ratio deals with capital stock or infrastructure of the country and compares it to the market value of corporate equity. When the market value of the Big Board is below replacement cost of corporate hard assets, you can rest assured the market is undervalued. For much of the eighties this was true. It spawned Mike Milken's hostile takeovers and the great-leveraged buyout scene that crested with the Kohlberg, Kravis, Roberts LBO of RJR Nabisco.

Today, the Q Ratio stands well over par, actually twice par (my estimate) which is why you only see discriminating deals done. Now, you can employ BB debt at 5%, not the 8% to 9% rate, late eighties. Valuation for everything, including art, real estate and gold boils down to your cost of carry, sooner or later.

Market bulls pooh-pooh Tobin as quaint and obsolete. How do you figure in Coca-Cola's trademark or an ethical drug house's patents - any serious intellectual achievement like cloud computing? This is valid, but Tobin is right, as well. His insight is based on how businesses are priced - fairly valued, overvalued or undervalued over successive cycles. It's a long-cycle reading that I file away but never discard from my apperceptive mass.

When I scanned the chart on the NASDAQ -100 Index, its V-shaped trajectory from the March 2020 low was over 60%, by summer. The S&P 500, also V-shaped, rose a solid 50%. Net, net, the market needs some consolidating between now and post-presidential election. When the dust settles, maybe yearend 2020, I expect my BB-rated bonds will have outperformed the S&P 500 Index. Year-to-date its total return is 5%. My high-yield portfolio is doing better sans the heartburn from the jitterbugging market.

Warren Buffett in the early nineties disposed of the "efficient market" in one sentence, referring to Black Monday when the index dropped 22%, overnight, and came near imploding, obviously inefficient. Never govern yourself by a dividend-discount model, either. Its moving parts wax too changeable - dividend payout ratios, earnings growth, inflation and interest rates.

A century's worth of market stats show even if you came in at the top of a cycle and stayed invested for at least a decade, your rate of return exceeds Treasury bills. This may be the situation right now. Historical memory is useful as a valuation tool for the market, but not for individual stocks which can sell anywhere.

What about price-earnings ratio comparisons? Going back over forty years my chart shows the trendline P/E for growth at 1.3 times the S&P 500. Currently, we're at a two-times ratio. This is a warning signal. The technology sector six years back was on parity with financials. Today it's two times that weighting. I'm thumbs down on banks, but if a Covid-19 vaccine is around the corner, banks are way underpriced.

If you are a growth-stock player, review 1972 when the sector peaked at 2.7 times market valuation. Then, the 1973 - 1974 recession destroyed growthies and they've never sold above two times the S&P 500 Index. The market traded at 18.4 times earnings during 1972 and then exceeded 22 times in 2000 and 17 times in 2014. So, a 20 multiple looks like the peak number. Economic cycles intervene and profit margins do get shaded when worldwide-competitive forces kick in.

Friends periodically ask me how long the good times last. Normally, I turn this question around and ask why they can't last. Consider, every central bank in the universe is praying for an inflationary bias. Until we see wage inflation and the end to easy money, stay invested.